The Life of

Thomas Campbell

Table of Contents

- Chronological Summary of Petrarch's Life.
- The Life of Petrarch.

List of Plates

- Petrarch.
- Castle of St. Angelo & St. Peters.
- Solitudes of Vaucluse. ("Fort de Bard", by James Duffield Harding (1797-1863))
- Santa Lucia, Naples. Artist: James Duffield Harding (1797-1863).
- Selva Piana, near Parma.
- Nice, Coast of Genoa. Artist: James Duffield Harding (1797-1863).
- Coast of Genoa.
- Bridge of Sighs,--Venice.
- Vicenza.
- Albenga, Coast of Genoa. Artist: James Duffield Harding (1797-1863).
- Milan Cathedral.
- The Library of St. Mark, St. Mark's Place, Venice.
- Ferrara.
- Petrarch's house at Arquà.
- Avignon.

Petrarch.

CHRONOLOGICAL SUMMARY OF PETRARCH'S LIFE.

A.D.		PAGE
1304.	Born at Arezzo, the 20th of July.	ix
1305.	Is taken to Incisa at the age of seven months, where he remains seven years.	x
1312.	Is removed to Pisa, where he remains seven months.	x
1313.	Accompanies his parents to Avignon.	xi
1315.	Goes to live at Carpentras.	xi
1319.	Is sent to Montpelier.	xi
1323.	Is removed to Bologna.	xii
1326.	Returns to Avignon—loses his parents—contracts a friendship with James Colonna.	xiii
1327.	Falls in love with Laura.	xvii
1330.	Goes to Lombes with James Colonna—forms acquaintance with Socrates and Lælius—and returns to Avignon to live in the house of Cardinal Colonna.	xviii
1331.	Travels to Paris—travels through Flanders and Brabant, and visits a part of Germany.	xxiv
1333.	His first journey to Rome—his long navigation as far as the coast of England—his return to Avignon.	xxxiii
1337.	Birth of his son John—he retires to Vaucluse.	xxxv
1339.	Commences writing his epic poem, "Africa."	xxxviii
1340.	Receives an invitation from Rome to come and be crowned as Laureate —and another invitation, to the same effect, from Paris.	xlii
1341.	Goes to Naples, and thence to Rome, where he is crowned in the Capitol—repairs to Parma—death of Tommaso da Messina and James Colonna.	xliii
1342.	Goes as orator of the Roman people to Clement VI. at Avignon—Studies the Greek language under Barlaamo.	xlviii
1343.	Birth of his daughter Francesca—he writes his dialogues "De secreto conflictu curarum suarum"—is sent to Naples by Clement VI. and Cardinal Colonna—goes to Rome for a third and a fourth time—returns from Naples to Parma.	li
1344.	Continues to reside in Parma.	lviii
1345.	Leaves Parma, goes to Bologna, and thence to Verona—returns to Avignon.	lviii
1346.	Continues to live at Avignon—is elected canon of Parma.	lix
1347.	Revolution at Rome—Petrarch's connection with the Tribune—takes his fifth journey to Italy—repairs to Parma.	lxiv
1348.	Goes to Verona—death of Laura—he returns again to Parma—his autograph memorandum in the Milan copy of Virgil—visits Manfredi, Lord of Carpi, and James Carrara at Padua.	lxvii

1349. Goes from Parma to Mantua and Ferrara—returns to Padua, and receives, probably in this year, a canonicate in Padua.	lxxiii
1350. Is raised to the Archdeaconry of Parma—writes to the Emperor Charles IV.—goes to Rome, and, in going and returning, stops at Florence.	lxxiii
1351. Writes to Andrea Dandolo with a view to reconcile the Venetians and Florentines—the Florentines decree the restoration of his paternal property, and send John Boccaccio to recall him to his country—he returns, for the sixth time, to Avignon—is consulted by the four Cardinals, who had been deputed to reform the government of Rome.	lxxx
1352. Writes to Clement VI. the letter which excites against him the enmity of the medical tribe—begins writing his treatise "De Vita Solitaria."	lxxxvii
1353. Visits his brother in the Carthusian monastery of Monte Rivo—writes his treatise "De Otio Religiosorum"—returns to Italy—takes up his abode with the Visconti—is sent by the Archbishop Visconti to Venice, to negotiate a peace between the Venetians and Genoese.	xc
1354. Visits the Emperor at Mantua.	xcix
1355. His embassy to the Emperor—publishes his "Invective against a Physician."	xcix
1360. His embassy to John, King of France.	cxii
1361. Leaves Milan and settles at Venice—gives his library to the Venetians.	cxiii
1364. Writes for Lucchino del Verme his treatise "De Officio et Virtutibus Imperatoris."	cxvii
1366. Writes to Urban V. imploring him to remove the Papal residence to Rome—finishes his treatise "De Remediis utriusque Fortunæ."	cxviii
1368. Quits Venice—four young Venetians, either in this year or the preceding, promulgate a critical judgment against Petrarch—repairs to Pavia to negotiate peace between the Pope's Legate and the Visconti.	cxix
1370. Sets out to visit the Pontiff—is taken ill at Ferrara—retires to Arquà among the Euganean hills.	cxxii
1371. Writes his "Invectiva contra Gallum," and his "Epistle to Posterity."	cxxiii
1372. Writes for Francesco da Carrara his essay "De Republica optime administranda."	cxxx
1373. Is sent to Venice by Francesco da Carrara.	cxxx
1374. Translates the Griseldis of Boccaccio—dies on the 18th of July in the same year.	cxxxi

The Life of Petrarch.

The family of Petrarch was originally of Florence, where his ancestors held employments of trust and honour. Garzo, his great-grandfather, was a notary universally respected for his integrity and judgment. Though he had never devoted himself exclusively to letters, his literary opinion was consulted by men of learning. He lived to be a hundred and four years old, and died, like Plato, in the same bed in which he had been born.

Garzo left three sons, one of whom was the grandfather of Petrarch. Diminutives being customary to the Tuscan tongue, Pietro, the poet's father, was familiarly called Petracco, or little Peter. He, like his ancestors, was a notary, and not undistinguished for sagacity. He had several important commissions from government. At last, in the increasing conflicts between the Guelphs and the Ghibellines—or, as they now called themselves, the Blacks and the Whites—Petracco, like Dante, was obliged to fly from his native city, along with the other Florentines of the White party. He was unjustly accused of having officially issued a false deed, and was condemned, on the 20th of October, 1302, to pay a fine of one thousand lire, and to have his hand cut off, if that sum was not paid within ten days from the time he should be apprehended. Petracco fled, taking with him his wife, Eletta Canigiani, a lady of a distinguished family in Florence, several of whom had held the office of Gonfalonier.

Petracco and his wife first settled at Arezzo, a very ancient city of Tuscany. Hostilities did not cease between the Florentine factions till some years afterwards; and, in an attempt made by the Whites to take Florence by assault, Petracco was present with his party. They were repulsed. This action, which was fatal to their cause, took place in the night between the 19th and 20th days of July, 1304,—the precise date of the birth of Petrarch.

During our poet's infancy, his family had still to struggle with an adverse fate; for his proscribed and wandering father was obliged to separate himself from his wife and child, in order to have the means of supporting them.

As the pretext for banishing Petracco was purely personal, Eletta, his wife, was not included in the sentence. She removed to a small property of her husband's, at Ancisa, fourteen miles from Florence, and took the little poet along with her, in the seventh month of his age. In their passage thither, both mother and child, together with their guide, had a narrow escape from being drowned in the Arno. Eletta entrusted her precious charge to a robust peasant, who, for fear of hurting the child, wrapt it in a swaddling cloth, and suspended it over his shoulder, in the same manner as Metabus is described by Virgil, in the eleventh book of the Æneid, to have carried his daughter Camilla. In passing the river, the horse of the guide, who carried Petrarch, stumbled, and sank down; and in their struggles to save him, both his sturdy bearer and the frantic parent were, like the infant itself, on the point of being drowned.

After Eletta had settled at Ancisa, Petracco often visited her by stealth, and the pledges of their affection were two other sons, one of whom died in childhood. The other, called Gherardo, was educated along with Petrarch. Petrarch remained with his mother at Ancisa for seven years.

The arrival of the Emperor, Henry VII., in Italy, revived the hopes of the banished Florentines; and Petracco, in order to wait the event, went to Pisa, whither he brought his wife and Francesco, who was now in his eighth year. Petracco remained with his family in Pisa for several months; but tired at last of fallacious hopes, and not daring to trust himself to the promises of the popular party, who offered to recall him to Florence, he sought an asylum in Avignon, a place to which many Italians were allured by the hopes of honours and gain at the papal residence. In this voyage, Petracco and his family were nearly shipwrecked off Marseilles.

But the numbers that crowded to Avignon, and its luxurious court, rendered that city an uncomfortable place for a family in slender circumstances. Petracco accordingly removed his household, in 1315, to Carpentras, a small quiet town, where living was cheaper than at Avignon. There, under the care of his mother, Petrarch imbibed his first instruction, and was taught by one Convennole da Prato as much grammar and logic as could be learned at his age, and more than could be learned by an ordinary disciple from so common-place a preceptor. This poor master, however, had sufficient intelligence to appreciate the genius of Petrarch, whom he esteemed and honoured beyond all his other pupils. On the other hand, his illustrious scholar aided him, in his old age and poverty, out of his scanty income.

Petrarch used to compare Convennole to a whetstone, which is blunt itself, but which sharpens others. His old master, however was sharp enough to overreach him in the matter of borrowing and lending. When the poet had collected a considerable library, Convennole paid him a visit, and, pretending to be engaged in something that required him to consult Cicero, borrowed a copy of one of the works of that orator, which was particularly valuable. He made excuses, from time to time, for not returning it; but Petrarch, at last, had too good reason to suspect that the old grammarian had pawned it. The poet would willingly have paid for redeeming it, but Convennole was so much ashamed, that he would not tell to whom it was pawned; and the precious manuscript was lost.

Petracco contracted an intimacy with Settimo, a Genoese, who was like himself, an exile for his political principles, and who fixed his abode at Avignon with his wife and his boy, Guido Settimo, who was about the same age with Petrarch. The two youths formed a friendship, which subsisted between them for life.

Petrarch manifested signs of extraordinary sensibility to the charms of nature in his childhood, both when he was at Carpentras and at Avignon. One day, when he was at the latter residence, a party was made up, to see the fountain of Vaucluse, a few leagues from Avignon. The little Francesco had no sooner arrived at the lovely landscape than he was struck with its beauties, and exclaimed, "Here, now, is a retirement suited to my taste, and preferable, in my eyes, to the greatest and most splendid cities."

A genius so fine as that of our poet could not servilely confine itself to the slow method of school learning, adapted to the intellects of ordinary boys. Accordingly, while his fellow pupils were still plodding through the first rudiments of Latin, Petrarch had recourse to the original writers, from whom the grammarians drew their authority, and particularly employed himself in perusing the works of Cicero. And, although he was, at this time, much too young to comprehend the full force of the orator's reasoning, he was so struck with the charms of his style, that he considered him the only true model in prose composition.

His father, who was himself something of a scholar, was pleased and astonished at this early proof of his good taste; he applauded his classical studies, and encouraged him to persevere in them; but, very soon, he imagined that he had cause to repent of his commendations. Classical learning was, in that age, regarded as a mere solitary accomplishment, and the law was the only road that led to honours and preferment. Petracco was, therefore, desirous to turn into that channel the brilliant qualities of his son; and for this purpose he sent him, at the age of fifteen, to the university of Montpelier. Petrarch remained there for four years, and attended lectures on law from some of the most famous professors of the science. But his prepossession for Cicero prevented him from much frequenting the dry and dusty walks of jurisprudence. In his epistle to posterity, he endeavours to justify this repugnance by other motives. He represents the abuses, the chicanery, and mercenary practices of the law, as inconsistent with every principle of candour and honesty.

When Petracco observed that his son made no great progress in his legal studies at Montpelier, he removed him, in 1323, to Bologna, celebrated for the study of the canon and civil law, probably imagining that the superior fame of the latter place might attract him to love the law. To Bologna Petrarch was accompanied by his brother Gherardo, and by his inseparable friend, young Guido Settimo.

But neither the abilities of the several professors in that celebrated academy, nor the strongest exhortations of his father, were sufficient to conquer the deeply-rooted aversion which our poet had conceived for the law. Accordingly, Petracco hastened to Bologna, that he might endeavour to check his son's indulgence in literature, which disconcerted his favourite designs. Petrarch, guessing at the motive of his arrival, hid the copies of Cicero, Virgil, and some other authors, which composed his small library, and to purchase which he had deprived himself of almost the necessaries of life. His father, however, soon discovered the place of their concealment, and threw them into the fire. Petrarch exhibited as much agony as if he had been himself the martyr of his father's resentment. Petracco was so much affected by his son's tears, that he rescued from the flames Cicero and Virgil, and, presenting them to Petrarch, he said, "Virgil will console you for the loss of your other MSS., and Cicero will prepare you for the study of the law."

It is by no means wonderful that a mind like Petrarch's could but ill relish the glosses of the Code and the commentaries on the Decretals.

At Bologna, however, he met with an accomplished literary man and no inelegant poet in one of the professors, who, if he failed in persuading Petrarch to make the law his profession, certainly quickened his relish and ambition for poetry. This man was Cino da Pistoia, who is esteemed by Italians as the most tender and harmonious lyric poet in the native language anterior to Petrarch.

During his residence at Bologna, Petrarch made an excursion as far as Venice, a city that struck him with enthusiastic admiration. In one of his letters he calls it "*orbem alterum.*" Whilst Italy was harassed, he says, on all sides by continual dissensions, like the sea in a storm, Venice alone appeared like a safe harbour, which overlooked the tempest without feeling its commotion. The resolute and independent spirit of that republic made an indelible impression on Petrarch's heart. The young poet, perhaps, at this time little imagined that Venice was to be the last scene of his triumphant eloquence.

Soon after his return from Venice to Bologna, he received the melancholy intelligence of the death of his mother, in the thirty-eighth year of her age. Her age is known by a copy of verses which Petrarch wrote upon her death, the verses being the same in number as the years of her life. She had lived humble and retired, and had devoted herself to the good of her family; virtuous amidst the prevalence of corrupted manners, and, though a beautiful woman, untainted by the breath of calumny. Petrarch has repaid her maternal affection by preserving her memory from oblivion. Petracco did not long survive the death of this excellent woman. According to the judgment of our poet, his father was a man of strong character and understanding. Banished from his native country, and engaged in providing for his family, he was prevented by the scantiness of his fortune, and the cares of his situation, from rising to that eminence which he might have otherwise attained. But his admiration of

Cicero, in an age when that author was universally neglected, was a proof of his superior mind.

Petrarch quitted Bologna upon the death of his father, and returned to Avignon, with his brother Gherardo, to collect the shattered remains of their father's property. Upon their arrival, they found their domestic affairs in a state of great disorder, as the executors of Petracco's will had betrayed the trust reposed in them, and had seized most of the effects of which they could dispose. Under these circumstances, Petrarch was most anxious for a MS. of Cicero, which his father had highly prized. "The guardians," he writes, "eager to appropriate what they esteemed the more valuable effects, had fortunately left this MS. as a thing of no value." Thus he owed to their ignorance this treatise, which he considered the richest portion of the inheritance left him by his father.

But, that inheritance being small, and not sufficient for the maintenance of the two brothers, they were obliged to think of some profession for their subsistence; they therefore entered the church; and Avignon was the place, of all others, where preferment was most easily obtained. John XXII. had fixed his residence entirely in that city since October, 1316, and had appropriated to himself the nomination to all the vacant benefices. The pretence for this appropriation was to prevent simony—in others, not in his Holiness—as the sale of benefices was carried by him to an enormous height. At every promotion to a bishopric, he removed other bishops; and, by the meanest impositions, soon amassed prodigious wealth. Scandalous emoluments, also, which arose from the sale of indulgences, were enlarged, if not invented, under his papacy, and every method of acquiring riches was justified which could contribute to feed his avarice. By these sordid means, he collected such sums, that, according to Villani, he left behind him, *in the sacred treasury*, twenty-five millions of florins, a treasure which Voltaire remarks is hardly credible.

The luxury and corruption which reigned in the Roman court at Avignon are fully displayed in some letters of Petrarch's, without either date or address. The partizans of that court, it is true, accuse him of prejudice and exaggeration. He painted, as they allege, the popes and cardinals in the gloomiest colouring. His letters contain the blackest catalogue of crimes that ever disgraced humanity.

Petrarch was twenty-two years of age when he settled at Avignon, a scene of licentiousness and profligacy. The luxury of the cardinals, and the pomp and riches of the papal court, were displayed in an extravagant profusion of feasts and ceremonies, which attracted to Avignon women of all ranks, among whom intrigue and gallantry were generally countenanced. Petrarch was by nature of a warm temperament, with vivid and susceptible passions, and strongly attached to the fair sex. We must not therefore be surprised if, with these dispositions, and in such a dissolute city, he was betrayed into some excesses. But these were the result of his complexion, and not of deliberate profligacy. He alludes to this subject in his Epistle to Posterity, with every appearance of truth and candour.

From his own confession, Petrarch seems to have been somewhat vain of his personal appearance during his youth, a venial foible, from which neither the handsome nor the homely, nor the wise nor the foolish, are exempt. It is amusing to find our own Milton betraying this weakness, in spite of all the surrounding strength of his character. In answering one of his slanderers, who had called him pale and cadaverous, the author of Paradise Lost appeals to all who knew him whether his complexion was not so fresh and blooming as to make him appear ten years younger than he really was.

Petrarch, when young, was so strikingly handsome, that he was frequently pointed at and admired as he passed along, for his features were manly, well-formed, and expressive, and his carriage was graceful and distinguished. He was sprightly in conversation, and his voice was uncommonly musical. His complexion was between brown and fair, and his eyes were bright and animated. His countenance was a faithful index of his heart.

He endeavoured to temper the warmth of his constitution by the regularity of his living and the plainness of his diet. He indulged little in either wine or sleep, and fed chiefly on fruits and vegetables.

In his early days he was nice and neat in his dress, even to a degree of affectation, which, in later life, he ridiculed when writing to his brother Gherardo. "Do you remember," he says, "how much care we employed in the lure of dressing our persons; when we traversed the streets, with what attention did we not avoid every breath of wind which might discompose our hair; and with what caution did we not prevent the least speck of dirt from soiling our garments!"

This vanity, however, lasted only during his youthful days. And even then neither attention to his personal appearance, nor his attachment to the fair sex, nor his attendance upon the great, could induce Petrarch to neglect his own mental improvement, for, amidst all these occupations, he found leisure for application, and devoted himself to the cultivation of his favourite pursuits of literature.

Inclined by nature to moral philosophy, he was guided by the reading of Cicero and Seneca to that profound knowledge of the human heart, of the duties of others and of our own duties, which shows itself in all his writings. Gifted with a mind full of enthusiasm for poetry, he learned from Virgil elegance and dignity in versification. But he had still higher advantages from the perusal of Livy. The magnanimous actions of Roman heroes so much excited the soul of Petrarch, that he thought the men of his own age light and contemptible.

His first compositions were in Latin: many motives, however, induced him to compose in the vulgar tongue, as Italian was then called, which, though improved by Dante, was still, in many respects, harsh and inelegant, and much in want of new beauties. Petrarch wrote for the living, and for that portion of the living who were least of all to be fascinated by the language of the dead. Latin might be all very well for inscriptions on mausoleums, but it was not suited for the ears of beauty and the bowers of love. The Italian language acquired, under his cultivation, increased elegance and richness, so that the harmony of his style has contributed to its beauty. He did not, however, attach himself solely to Italian, but composed much in Latin, which he reserved for graver, or, as he considered, more important subjects. His compositions in Latin are—Africa, an epic poem; his Bucolics, containing twelve eclogues; and three books of epistles.

Petrarch's greatest obstacles to improvement arose from the scarcity of authors whom he wished to consult—for the manuscripts of the writers of the Augustan age were, at that time, so uncommon, that many could not be procured, and many more of them could not be purchased under the most extravagant price. This scarcity of books had checked the dawning light of literature. The zeal of our poet, however, surmounted all these obstacles, for he was indefatigable in collecting and copying many of the choicest manuscripts; and posterity is indebted to him for the possession of many valuable writings, which were in danger of being lost through the carelessness or ignorance of the possessors.

Petrarch could not but perceive the superiority of his own understanding and the brilliancy of his abilities. The modest humility which knows not its own worth is not wont to show itself in minds much above mediocrity; and to elevated geniuses this virtue is a stranger. Petrarch from his youthful age had an internal assurance that he should prove worthy of estimation and honours. Nevertheless, as he advanced in the field of science, he saw the prospect increase, Alps over Alps, and seemed to be lost amidst the immensity of objects before him. Hence the anticipation of immeasurable labours occasionally damped his application. But from this depression of spirits he was much relieved by the encouragement of John of Florence, one of the secretaries of the Pope, a man of learning and probity. He soon distinguished the extraordinary abilities of Petrarch; he directed him in his studies, and cheered up his ambition. Petrarch returned his affection with unbounded confidence. He entrusted him with all his foibles, his disgusts, and his uneasinesses. He says that he never conversed with him without finding himself more calm and composed, and more animated for study.

The superior sagacity of our poet, together with his pleasing manners, and his increasing reputation for knowledge, ensured to him the most flattering prospects of success. His conversation was courted by men of rank, and his acquaintance was sought by men of learning. It was at this time, 1326, that his merit procured him the friendship and patronage of James Colonna, who belonged to one of the most ancient and illustrious families of Italy.

"About the twenty-second year of my life," Petrarch writes to one of his friends, "I became acquainted with James Colonna. He had seen me whilst I resided at Bologna, and was prepossessed, as he was pleased to say, with my appearance. Upon his arrival at Avignon, he again saw me, when, having inquired minutely into the state of my affairs, he admitted me to his friendship. I cannot sufficiently describe the cheerfulness of his temper, his social disposition, his moderation in prosperity, his constancy in adversity. I speak not from report, but from my own experience. He was endowed with a persuasive and forcible eloquence. His conversation and letters displayed the amiableness of his sincere character. He gained the first place in my affections, which he ever afterwards retained."

Such is the portrait which our poet gives of James Colonna. A faithful and wise friend is among the most precious gifts of fortune; but, as friendships cannot wholly feed our affections, the heart of Petrarch, at this ardent age, was destined to be swayed by still tenderer feelings. He had nearly finished his twenty-third year without having ever seriously known the passion of love. In that year he first saw Laura. Concerning this lady, at one time, when no life of Petrarch had been yet written that was not crude and inaccurate, his biographers launched into the wildest speculations. One author considered her as an allegorical being; another discovered her to be a type of the Virgin Mary; another thought her an allegory of poetry and repentance. Some denied her even allegorical existence, and deemed her a mere phantom beauty, with which the poet had fallen in love, like Pygmalion with the work of his own creation. All these caprices about Laura's history have been long since dissipated, though the principal facts respecting her were never distinctly verified, till De Sade, her own descendant, wrote his memoirs of the Life of Petrarch.

Petrarch himself relates that in 1327, exactly at the first hour of the 6th of April, he first beheld Laura in the church of St. Clara of Avignon,[1] where neither the sacredness of the place, nor the solemnity of the day, could prevent him from being smitten for life with human love. In that fatal hour he saw a lady, a little younger than himself[2] in a green mantle sprinkled with violets, on which her golden hair fell plaited in tresses. She was distinguished from all others by her proud and delicate carriage. The impression which she made on his heart was sudden, yet it was never effaced.

Laura, descended from a family of ancient and noble extraction, was the daughter of Audibert de Noves, a Provençal nobleman, by his wife Esmessenda. She was born at Avignon, probably in 1308. She had a considerable fortune, and was married in 1325 to Hugh de Sade. The particulars of her life are little known, as Petrarch has left few traces of them in his letters; and it was still less likely that he should enter upon her personal history in his sonnets, which, as they were principally addressed to herself, made it unnecessary for him to inform her of what she already knew.

While many writers have erred in considering Petrarch's attachment as visionary, others, who have allowed the reality of his passion, have been mistaken in their opinion of its object. They allege that Petrarch was a happy lover, and that his mistress was accustomed to meet him at Vaucluse, and make him a full compensation for his fondness. No one at all acquainted with the life and writings of Petrarch will need to be told that this is an absurd fiction. Laura, a married woman, who bore ten children to a rather morose husband, could not have gone to meet him at Vaucluse without the most flagrant scandal. It is evident from his writings that she repudiated his passion whenever it threatened to exceed the limits of virtuous friendship. On one occasion, when he seemed to presume too far upon her favour, she said to him with severity, "I am not what you take me for." If his love had been successful, he would have said less about it.

Of the two persons in this love affair, I am more inclined to pity Laura than Petrarch. Independently of her personal charms, I cannot conceive Laura otherwise than as a kind-hearted, loveable woman, who could not well be supposed to be totally indifferent to the devotion of the most famous and fascinating man of his age. On the other hand, what was the penalty that she would have paid if she had encouraged his addresses as far as he would have carried them? Her disgrace, a stigma left on her family, and the loss of all that character which upholds a woman in her own estimation and in that of the world. I would not go so far as to say that she did not at times betray an anxiety to retain him under the spell of her fascination, as, for instance, when she is said to have cast her eyes to the ground in sadness when he announced his intention to leave Avignon; but still I should like to hear her own explanation before I condemned her. And, after all, she was only anxious for the continuance of attentions, respecting which she had made a fixed understanding that they should not exceed the bounds of innocence.

We have no distinct account how her husband regarded the homage of Petrarch to his wife—whether it flattered his vanity, or moved his wrath. As tradition gives him no very good character for temper, the latter supposition is the more probable. Every morning that he went out he might hear from some kind friend the praises of a new sonnet which Petrarch had written on his wife; and, when he came back to dinner, of course his good humour was not improved by the intelligence. He was in the habit of scolding her till she wept; he married seven months after her death, and, from all that is known of him, appears to have been a bad husband. I suspect that Laura paid dearly for her poet's idolatry.

No incidents of Petrarch's life have been transmitted to us for the first year or two after his attachment to Laura commenced. He seems to have continued at Avignon, prosecuting his studies and feeding his passion.

James Colonna, his friend and patron, was promoted in 1328 to the bishopric of Lombes in Gascony; and in the year 1330 he went from Avignon to take possession of his diocese, and invited Petrarch to accompany him to his residence. No invitation could be more acceptable to our poet: they set out at the end of March, 1330. In order to reach Lombes, it was necessary to cross the whole of Languedoc, and to pass through Montpelier, Narbonne, and Toulouse. Petrarch already knew Montpelier, where he had, or ought to have, studied the law for four years.

Full of enthusiasm for Rome, Petrarch was rejoiced to find at Narbonne the city which had been the first Roman colony planted among the Gauls. This colony had been formed entirely of Roman citizens, and, in order to reconcile them to their exile, the city was built like a little image of Rome. It had its capital, its baths, arches, and fountains; all which works were worthy of the Roman name. In passing through Narbonne, Petrarch discovered a number of ancient monuments and inscriptions.

Our travellers thence proceeded to Toulouse, where they passed several days. This city, which was known even before the foundation of Rome, is called, in some ancient Roman acts, "Roma Garumnæ." It was famous in the classical ages for cultivating literature. After the fall of the Roman empire, the successive incursions of the Visigoths, the Saracens, and the Normans, for a long time silenced the Muses at Toulouse; but they returned to their favourite haunt after ages of barbarism had passed away. De Sade says, that what is termed Provençal poetry was much more cultivated by the Languedocians than by the Provençals, properly so called. The city of Toulouse was considered as the principal seat of this earliest modern poetry, which was carried to perfection in the twelfth and thirteenth centuries, under the patronage of the Counts of Toulouse, particularly Raimond V., and his son, Raimond VI. Petrarch speaks with high praise of those poets in his Triumphs of Love. It has been alleged that he owed them this mark of his regard for their having been so useful to him in his Italian poetry; and Nostradamus even accuses him of having stolen much from them. But Tassoni, who understood the Provençal poets better than Nostradamus, defends him successfully from this absurd accusation.

Although Provençal poetry was a little on its decline since the days of the Dukes of Aquitaine and the Counts of Toulouse, it was still held in honour; and, when Petrarch arrived, the Floral games had been established at Toulouse during six years.[3]

Ere long, however, our travellers found less agreeable objects of curiosity, that formed a sad contrast with the chivalric manners, the floral games, and the gay poetry of southern France. Bishop Colonna and Petrarch had intended to remain for some time at Toulouse; but their sojourn was abridged by their horror at a tragic event[4] in the principal monastery of the place. There lived in that monastery a young monk, named Augustin, who was expert in music, and accompanied the psalmody of the religious brothers with beautiful touches on the organ. The superior of the convent, relaxing its discipline, permitted Augustin frequently to mix with the world, in order to teach music, and to improve himself in the art. The young monk was in the habit of familiarly visiting the house of a respectable citizen: he was frequently in the society of his daughter, and, by the express encouragement of her father, undertook to exercise her in the practice of music. Another young man, who was in love with the girl, grew jealous of the monk, who was allowed to converse so familiarly with her, whilst he, her lay admirer, could only have stolen glimpses of her as she passed to church or to public spectacles. He set about the ruin of his supposed rival with cunning atrocity; and, finding that the young woman was infirm in health, suborned a physician, as worthless as himself, to declare that she was pregnant. Her credulous father, without inquiring whether the intelligence was true or false, went to the superior of the convent, and accused Augustin, who, though thunderstruck at the accusation, denied it firmly, and defended himself intrepidly. But the superior was deaf to his plea of innocence, and ordered him to be shut up in his cell, that he might await his punishment. Thither the poor young man was conducted, and threw himself on his bed in a state of horror.

The superior and the elders among the friars thought it a meet fate for the accused that he should be buried alive in a subterranean dungeon, after receiving the terrific sentence of *"Vade in pace."* At the end of several days the victim dashed out his brains against the walls of his sepulchre. Bishop Colonna, who, it would appear, had no power to oppose this hideous transaction, when he was informed of it, determined to leave the place immediately; and Petrarch in his indignation exclaimed—

> "Heu! fuge crudeles terras, fuge littus avarum."
>
> Virg.

On the 26th of May, 1330, the Bishop of Lombes and Petrarch quitted Toulouse, and arrived at the mansion of the diocese. Lombes—in Latin, Lombarium—lies at the foot of the Pyrenees, only eight leagues from Toulouse. It is small and ill-built, and offers no allurement to the curiosity of the traveller. Till lately it had been a simple abbey of the Augustine monks. The whole of the clergy of the little city, singing psalms, issued out of Lombes to meet their new pastor, who, under a rich canopy, was conducted to the principal church, and there, in his episcopal robes, blessed the people, and delivered an eloquent discourse. Petrarch beheld with admiration the dignified behaviour of the youthful prelate. James Colonna, though accustomed to the wealth and luxury of Rome, came to the Pyrenean rocks with a pleased countenance. "His aspect," says Petrarch, "made it seem as if Italy had been transported into Gascony." Nothing is more beautiful than the patient endurance of our destiny; yet there are many priests who would suffer translation to a well-paid, though mountainous bishopric, with patience and piety.

The vicinity of the Pyrenees renders the climate of Lombes very severe; and the character and conversation of the inhabitants were scarcely more genial than their climate. But Petrarch found in the bishop's abode friends who consoled him in this exile among the Lombesians. Two young and familiar inmates of the Bishop's house attracted and returned his attachment. The first of these was Lello di Stefani, a youth of a noble and ancient family in Rome, long attached to the Colonnas. Lello's gifted understanding was improved by study; so Petrarch tells us; and he could have been no ordinary man whom our accomplished poet so highly valued. In his youth he had quitted his studies for the profession of arms; but the return of peace restored him to his literary pursuits. Such was the attachment between Petrarch and Lello, that Petrarch gave him the name of Lælius, the most attached companion of Scipio. The other friend to whom Petrarch attached himself in the house of James Colonna was a young German, extremely accomplished in music. De Sade says that his name was Louis, without mentioning his cognomen. He was a native of Ham, near Bois le Duc, on the left bank of the Rhine between Brabant and Holland. Petrarch, with his Italian prejudices, regarded him as a barbarian by birth; but he was so fascinated by his serene temper and strong judgment, that he singled him out to be the chief of all his friends, and gave him the name of Socrates, noting him as an example that Nature can sometimes produce geniuses in the most unpropitious regions.

After having passed the summer of 1330 at Lombes, the Bishop returned to Avignon, in order to meet his father, the elder Stefano Colonna, and his brother the Cardinal.

The Colonnas were a family of the first distinction in modern Italy. They had been exceedingly powerful during the popedom of Boniface VIII., through the talents of the late Cardinal James Colonna, brother of the famous old Stefano, so well known to Petrarch, and whom he used to call a phœnix sprung up from the ashes of Rome. Their house possessed also an influential public character in the Cardinal Pietro, brother of the younger Stefano. They were formidable from the territories and castles which they possessed, and by their alliance and friendship with Charles, King of Naples. The power of the Colonna family became offensive to Boniface, who, besides, hated the two Cardinals for having opposed the renunciation of Celestine V., which Boniface had fraudulently obtained. Boniface procured a crusade against them. They were beaten, expelled from their castles, and almost exterminated; they implored peace, but in vain; they were driven from Rome, and obliged to seek refuge, some in Sicily and others in France. During the time of their exile, Boniface proclaimed it a capital crime to give shelter to any of them.

The Colonnas finally returned to their dignities and property, and afterwards made successful war against the house of their rivals, the Orsini.

John Colonna, the Cardinal, brother of the Bishop of Lombes, and son of old Stefano, was one of the very ablest men at the papal court. He insisted on our poet taking up his abode in his own palace at Avignon. "What good fortune was this for me!" says Petrarch. "This great man never made me feel that he was my superior in station. He was like a father or an indulgent brother; and I lived in his house as if it had been my own." At a subsequent period, we find him on somewhat cooler terms with John Colonna, and complaining that his domestic dependence had, by length of time, become wearisome to him. But great allowance is to be made for such apparent inconsistencies in human attachment. At different times our feelings and language on any subject may be different without being insincere. The truth seems to be that Petrarch looked forward to the friendship of the Colonnas for promotion, which he either received scantily, or not at all; so it is little marvellous if he should have at last felt the tedium of patronage.

For the present, however, this home was completely to Petrarch's taste. It was the rendezvous of all strangers distinguished by their knowledge and talents, whom the papal court attracted to Avignon, which was now the great centre of all political negotiations.

This assemblage of the learned had a powerful influence on Petrarch's fine imagination. He had been engaged for some time in the perusal of Livy, and his enthusiasm for ancient Rome was heightened, if possible, by the conversation of old Stefano Colonna, who dwelt on no subject with so much interest as on the temples and palaces of the ancient city, majestic even in their ruins.

During the bitter persecution raised against his family by Boniface VIII., Stefano Colonna had been the chief object of the Pope's implacable resentment. Though oppressed by the most adverse circumstances, his estates confiscated, his palaces levelled with the ground, and himself driven into exile, the majesty of his appearance, and the magnanimity of his character, attracted the respect of strangers wherever he went. He had the air of a sovereign prince rather than of an exile, and commanded more regard than monarchs in the height of their ostentation.

In the picture of his times, Stefano makes a noble and commanding figure. If the reader, however, happens to search into that period of Italian history, he will find many facts to cool the romance of his imagination respecting all the Colonna family. They were, in plain truth, an oppressive aristocratic family. The portion of Italy which they and their tyrannical rivals possessed was infamously governed. The highways were rendered impassable by banditti, who were in the pay of contesting feudal lords; and life and property were everywhere insecure.

Stefano, nevertheless, seems to have been a man formed for better times. He improved in the school of misfortune—the serenity of his temper remained unclouded by adversity, and his faculties unimpaired by age.

Among the illustrious strangers who came to Avignon at this time was our countryman, Richard de Bury, then accounted the most learned man of England. He arrived at Avignon in 1331, having been sent to the Pope by Edward III. De Sade conceives that the object of his embassy was to justify his sovereign before the Pontiff for having confined the Queen-mother in the castle of Risings, and for having caused her favourite, Roger de Mortimer, to be hanged. It was a matter of course that so illustrious a stranger as Richard de Bury should be received with distinction by Cardinal Colonna. Petrarch eagerly seized the opportunity of forming his acquaintance, confident that De Bury could give him valuable information on many points of geography and history. They had several conversations. Petrarch tells us that he entreated the learned Englishman to make him acquainted with the true situation of the isle of Thule, of which the ancients speak with much uncertainty, but which their best geographers place at the distance of some days' navigation from the north of England. De Bury was, in all probability, puzzled with the question, though he did not like to confess his ignorance. He excused himself by promising to inquire into the subject as soon as he should get back to his books in England, and to write to him the best information he could afford. It does not appear, however, that he performed his promise.

De Bury's stay at the court of Avignon was very short. King Edward, it is true, sent him a second time to the Pope, two years afterwards, on important business. The seeds of discord between France and England began to germinate strongly, and that circumstance probably occasioned De Bury's second mission. Unfortunately, however, Petrarch could not avail himself of his return so as to have further interviews with the English scholar. Petrarch wrote repeatedly to De Bury for his promised explanations respecting Thule; but, whether our countryman had found nothing in his library to satisfy his inquiries, or was prevented by his public occupations, there is no appearance of his having ever answered Petrarch's letters.

Stephano Colonna the younger had brought with him to Avignon his son Agapito, who was destined for the church, that he might be educated under the eyes of the Cardinal and the Bishop, who were his uncles. These two prelates joined with their father in entreating Petrarch to undertake the superintendence of Agapito's studies. Our poet, avaricious of his time, and jealous of his independence, was at first reluctant to undertake the charge; but, from his attachment to the family, at last accepted it. De Sade tells us that Petrarch was not successful in the young man's education; and, from a natural partiality for the hero of his biography, lays the blame on his pupil. At the same time he acknowledges that a man with poetry in his head and love in his heart was not the most proper mentor in the world for a youth who was to be educated for the church. At this time, Petrarch's passion for Laura continued to haunt his peace with incessant violence. She had received him at first with good-humour and affability; but it was only while he set strict bounds to the expression of his attachment. He had not, however, sufficient self-command to comply with these terms. His constant assiduities, his eyes continually riveted upon her, and the wildness of his looks, convinced her of his inordinate attachment; her virtue took alarm; she retired whenever he approached her, and even covered her face with a veil whilst he was present, nor would she condescend to the slightest action or look that might seem to countenance his passion.

Petrarch complains of these severities in many of his melancholy sonnets. Meanwhile, if fame could have been a balm to love, he might have been happy. His reputation as a poet was increasing, and his compositions were read with universal approbation.

The next interesting event in our poet's life was a larger course of travels, which he took through the north of France, through Flanders, Brabant, and a part of Germany, subsequently to his tour in Languedoc. Petrarch mentions that he undertook this journey about the twenty-fifth year of his age. He was prompted to travel not only by his curiosity to observe men and manners, by his desire of seeing monuments of antiquity, and his hopes of discovering the MSS. of ancient authors, but also, we may believe, by his wish, if it were possible, to escape from himself, and to forget Laura.

From Paris Petrarch wrote as follows to Cardinal Colonna.

"I have visited Paris, the capital of the whole kingdom of France. I entered it in the same state of mind that was felt by Apuleias when he visited Hypata, a city of Thessaly, celebrated for its magic, of which such wonderful things were related, looking again and again at every object, in solicitous suspense, to know whether all that he had heard of the far-famed place was true or false. Here I pass a great deal of time in observation, and, as the day is too short for my curiosity, I add the night. At last, it seems to me that, by long exploring, I have enabled myself to distinguish between the true and the false in what is related about Paris. But, as the subject would be too tedious for this occasion, I shall defer entering fully into particulars till I can do so *vivâ voce*. My impatience, however, impels me to sketch for you briefly a general idea of this so celebrated city, and of the character of its inhabitants.

"Paris, though always inferior to its fame, and much indebted to the lies of its own people, is undoubtedly a great city. To be sure I never saw a dirtier place, except Avignon. At the same time, its population contains the most learned of men, and it is like a great basket in which are collected the rarest fruits of every country. From the time that its university was founded, as they say by Alcuin, the teacher of Charlemagne, there has not been, to my knowledge, a single Parisian of any fame. The great luminaries of the university were all strangers; and, if the love of my country does not deceive me, they were chiefly Italians, such as Pietro Lombardo, Tomaso d'Aquino, Bonaventura, and many others.

"The character of the Parisians is very singular. There was a time when, from the ferocity of their manners, the French were reckoned barbarians. At present the case is wholly changed. A gay disposition, love of society, ease, and playfulness in conversation now characterize them. They seek every opportunity of distinguishing themselves; and make war against all cares with joking, laughing, singing, eating, and drinking. Prone, however, as they are to pleasure, they are not heroic in adversity. The French love their country and their countrymen; they censure with rigour the faults of other nations, but spread a proportionably thick veil over their own defects."

From Paris, Petrarch proceeded to Ghent, of which only he makes mention to the Cardinal, without noticing any of the towns that lie between. It is curious to find our poet out of humour with Flanders on account of the high price of wine, which was not an indigenous article. In the latter part of his life, Petrarch was certainly one of the most abstemious of men; but, at this period, it would seem that he drank good liquor enough to be concerned about its price.

From Ghent he passed on to Liege. "This city is distinguished," he says, "by the riches and the number of its clergy. As I had heard that excellent MSS. might be found there, I stopped in the place for some time. But is it not singular that in so considerable a place I had difficulty to procure ink enough to copy two orations of Cicero's, and the little that I could obtain was as yellow as saffron?"

Petrarch was received at most of the places he visited, and more particularly at Cologne, with marks of great respect; and he was agreeably surprised to find that his reputation had acquired him the partiality and acquaintance of several inhabitants. He was conducted by his new friends to the banks of the Rhine, where the inhabitants were engaged in the performance of a superstitious annual ceremony, which, for its singularity, deserves to be recorded.

"The banks of the river were crowded with a considerable number of women, their persons comely, and their dress elegant. This great concourse of people seemed to create no confusion. A number of these women, with cheerful countenances, crowned with flowers, bathed their hands and arms in the stream, and uttered, at the same time, some harmonious expressions in a language which I did not understand. I inquired into the cause of this ceremony, and was informed that it arose from a tradition among the people, and particularly among the women, that the impending calamities of the year were carried away by this ablution, and that blessings succeeded in their place. Hence this ceremony is annually renewed, and the ablution performed with unremitting diligence."

The ceremony being finished, Petrarch smiled at their superstition, and exclaimed, "O happy inhabitants of the Rhine, whose waters wash out your miseries, whilst neither the Po nor the Tiber can wash out ours! You transmit your evils to the Britons by means of this river, whilst we send off ours to the Illyrians and the Africans. It seems that our rivers have a slower course."

Petrarch shortened his excursion that he might return the sooner to Avignon, where the Bishop of Lombes had promised to await his return, and take him to Rome.

When he arrived at Lyons, however, he was informed that the Bishop had departed from Avignon for Rome. In the first paroxysm of his disappointment he wrote a letter to his friend, which portrays strongly affectionate feelings, but at the same time an irascible temper. When he came to Avignon, the Cardinal Colonna relieved him from his irritation by acquainting him with the real cause of his brother's departure. The flames of civil dissension had been kindled at Rome between the rival families of Colonna and Orsini. The latter had made great preparations to carry on the war with vigour. In this crisis of affairs, James Colonna had been summoned to Rome to support the interests of his family, and, by his courage and influence, to procure them the succour which they so much required.

Petrarch continued to reside at Avignon for several years after returning from his travels in France and Flanders. It does not appear from his sonnets, during those years, either that his passion for Laura had abated, or that she had given him any more encouragement than heretofore. But in the year 1334, an accident renewed the utmost tenderness of his affections. A terrible affliction visited the city of Avignon. The heat and the drought were so excessive that almost the whole of the common people went about naked to the waist, and, with frenzy and miserable cries, implored Heaven to put an end to their calamities. Persons of both sexes and of all ages had their bodies covered with scales, and changed their skins like serpents.

Laura's constitution was too delicate to resist this infectious malady, and her illness greatly alarmed Petrarch. One day he asked her physician how she was, and was told by him that her condition was very dangerous: on that occasion he composed the following sonnet:[5]—

> This lovely spirit, if ordain'd to leave
> Its mortal tenement before its time,
> Heaven's fairest habitation shall receive
> And welcome her to breathe its sweetest clime.
> If she establish her abode between
> Mars and the planet-star of Beauty's queen,
> The sun will be obscured, so dense a cloud
> Of spirits from adjacent stars will crowd
> To gaze upon her beauty infinite.
> Say that she fixes on a lower sphere,
> Beneath the glorious sun, her beauty soon
> Will dim the splendour of inferior stars—
> Of Mars, of Venus, Mercury, and the Moon.
> She'll choose not Mars, but higher place than Mars;
> She will eclipse all planetary light,
> And Jupiter himself will seem less bright.

I trust that I have enough to say in favour of Petrarch to satisfy his rational admirers; but I quote this sonnet as an example of the worst style of Petrarch's poetry. I make the English reader welcome to rate my power of translating it at the very lowest estimation. He cannot go much further down than myself in the scale of valuation, especially if he has Italian enough to know that the exquisite mechanical harmony of Petrarch's style is beyond my reach. It has been alleged that this sonnet shows how much the mind of Petrarch had been influenced by his Platonic studies; but if Plato had written poetry he would never have been so extravagant.

Petrarch, on his return from Germany, had found the old Pope, John XXII., intent on two speculations, to both of which he lent his enthusiastic aid. One of them was a futile attempt to renew the crusades, from which Europe had reposed for a hundred years. The other was the transfer of the holy seat to Rome. The execution of this plan, for which Petrarch sighed as if it were to bring about the millennium, and which was not accomplished by another Pope without embroiling him with his Cardinals, was nevertheless more practicable than capturing Jerusalem. We are told by several Italian writers that the aged Pontiff, moved by repeated entreaties from the Romans, as well as by the remorse of his conscience, thought seriously of effecting this restoration; but the sincerity of his intentions is made questionable by the fact that he never fixed himself at Rome. He wrote, it is true, to Rome in 1333, ordering his palaces and gardens to be repaired; but the troubles which continued to agitate the city were alleged by him as too alarming for his safety there, and he repaired to Bologna to wait for quieter times.

On both of the above subjects, namely, the insane crusades and the more feasible restoration of the papal court to Rome, Petrarch wrote with devoted zeal; they are both alluded to in his twenty-second sonnet.

The death of John XXII. left the Cardinals divided into two great factions. The first was that of the French, at the head of which stood Cardinal Taillerand, son of the beautiful Brunissende de Foix, whose charms were supposed to have detained Pope Clement V. in France. The Italian Cardinals, who formed the opposite faction, had for their chief the Cardinal Colonna. The French party, being the more numerous, were, in some sort, masters of the election; they offered the tiara to Cardinal de Commenges, on condition that he would promise not to transfer the papal court to Rome. That prelate showed himself worthy of the dignity, by refusing to accept it on such terms.

To the surprise of the world, the choice of the conclave fell at last on James Founder, said to be the son of a baker at Savordun, who had been bred as a monk of Citeaux, and always wore the dress of the order. Hence he was called the White Cardinal. He was wholly unlike his portly predecessor John in figure and address, being small in stature, pale in complexion, and weak in voice. He expressed his own astonishment at the honour conferred on him, saying that they had elected an ass. If we may believe Petrarch, he did himself no injustice in likening himself to that quadruped; but our poet was somewhat harsh in his judgment of this Pontiff. He took the name of Benedict XII.

Shortly after his exaltation, Benedict received ambassadors from Rome, earnestly imploring him to bring back the sacred seat to their city; and Petrarch thought he could not serve the embassy better than by publishing a poem in Latin verse, exhibiting Rome in the character of a desolate matron imploring her husband to return to her. Benedict applauded the author of the epistle, but declined complying with its prayer. Instead of revisiting Italy, his Holiness ordered a magnificent and costly palace to be constructed for him at Avignon. Hitherto, it would seem that the Popes had lived in hired houses. In imitation of their Pontiff, the Cardinals set about building superb mansions, to the unbounded indignation of Petrarch, who saw in these new habitations not only a graceless and unchristian spirit of luxury, but a sure indication that their owners had no thoughts of removing to Rome.

In the January of the following year, Pope Benedict presented our poet with the canonicate of Lombes, with the expectancy of the first prebend which should become vacant. This preferment Petrarch is supposed to have owed to the influence of Cardinal Colonna.

The troubles which at this time agitated Italy drew to Avignon, in the year 1335, a personage who holds a pre-eminent interest in the life of Petrarch, namely, Azzo da Correggio, who was sent thither by the Scaligeri of Parma. The State of Parma had belonged originally to the popes; but two powerful families, the Rossis and the Correggios, had profited by the quarrels between the church and the empire to usurp the government, and during five-and-twenty years, Gilberto Correggio and Rolando Rossi alternately lost and won the sovereignty, till, at last, the confederate princes took the city, and conferred the government of it on Guido Correggio, the greatest enemy of the Rossis.

Gilbert Correggio left at his death a widow, the sister of Cane de la Scala, and four sons, Guido, Simone, Azzo, and Giovanni. It is only with Azzo that we are particularly concerned in the history of Petrarch.

Azzo was born in the year 1303, being thus a year older than our poet. Originally intended for the church, he preferred the sword to the crozier, and became a distinguished soldier. He married the daughter of Luigi Gonzagua, lord of Mantua. He was a man of bold original spirit, and so indefatigable that he acquired the name of Iron-foot. Nor was his energy merely physical; he read much, and forgot nothing—his memory was a library. Azzo's character, to be sure, even with allowance for turbulent times, is not invulnerable at all points to a rigid scrutiny; and, notwithstanding all the praises of Petrarch, who dedicated to him his Treatise on a Solitary Life in 1366, his political career contained some acts of perfidy. But we must inure ourselves, in the biography of Petrarch, to his over-estimation of favourites in the article of morals.

It was not long ere Petrarch was called upon to give a substantial proof of his regard for Azzo. After the seizure of Parma by the confederate princes, Marsilio di Rossi, brother of Rolando, went to Paris to demand assistance from the French king. The King of Bohemia had given over the government of Parma to him and his brothers, and the Rossi now saw it with grief assigned to his enemies, the Correggios. Marsilio could obtain no succour from the French, who were now busy in preparing for war with the English; so he carried to the Pope at Avignon his complaints against the alleged injustice of the lords of Verona and the Correggios in breaking an express treaty which they had made with the house of Rossi.

Azzo had the threefold task of defending, before the Pope's tribunal, the lords of Verona, whose envoy he was; the rights of his family, which were attacked; and his own personal character, which was charged with some grave objections. Revering the eloquence and influence of Petrarch, he importuned him to be his public defender. Our poet, as we have seen, had studied the law, but had never followed the profession. "It is not my vocation," he says, in his preface to his Familiar Epistles, "to undertake the defence of others. I detest the bar; I love retirement; I despise money; and, if I tried to let out my tongue for hire, my nature would revolt at the attempt."

But what Petrarch would not undertake either from taste or motives of interest, he undertook at the call of friendship. He pleaded the cause of Azzo before the Pope and Cardinals; it was a finely-interesting cause, that afforded a vast field for his eloquence. He brought off his client triumphantly; and the Rossis were defeated in their demand.

At the same time, it is a proud trait in Petrarch's character that he showed himself on this occasion not only an orator and a lawyer, but a perfect gentleman. In the midst of all his zealous pleading, he stooped neither to satire nor personality against the opposing party. He could say, with all the boldness of truth, in a letter to Ugolino di Rossi, the Bishop of Parma, "I pleaded against your house for Azzo Correggio, but you were present at the pleading; do me justice, and confess that I carefully avoided not only attacks on your family and reputation, but even those raillieries in which advocates so much delight."

On this occasion, Azzo had brought to Avignon, as his colleague in the lawsuit, Guglielmo da Pastrengo, who exercised the office of judge and notary at Verona. He was a man of deep knowledge in the law; versed, besides, in every branch of elegant learning, he was a poet into the bargain. In Petrarch's many books of epistles, there are few letters addressed by him to this personage; but it is certain that they contracted a friendship at this period which endured for life.

All this time the Bishop of Lombes still continued at Rome; and, from time to time, solicited his friend Petrarch to join him. "Petrarch would have gladly joined him," says De Sade; "but he was detained at Avignon by his attachment to John Colonna and his love of Laura:" a whimsical junction of detaining causes, in which the fascination of the Cardinal may easily be supposed to have been weaker than that of Laura. In writing to our poet, at Avignon, the Bishop rallied Petrarch on the imaginary existence of the object of his passion. Some stupid readers of the Bishop's letter, in subsequent times, took it into their heads that there was a literal proof in the prelate's jesting epistle of our poet's passion for Laura being a phantom and a fiction. But, possible as it may be, that the Bishop in reality suspected him to exaggerate the flame of his devotion for the two great objects of his idolatry, Laura and St. Augustine, he writes in a vein of pleasantry that need not be taken for grave accusation. "You are befooling us all, my dear Petrarch," says the prelate; "and it is wonderful that at so tender an age (Petrarch's tender age was at this time thirty-one) you can deceive the world with so much art and success. And, not content with deceiving the world, you would fain deceive Heaven itself. You make a semblance of loving St. Augustine and his works; but, in your heart, you love the poets and the philosophers. Your Laura is a phantom created by your imagination for the exercise of your poetry. Your verse, your love, your sighs, are all a fiction; or, if there is anything real in your passion, it is not for the lady Laura, but for the laurel—*that is*, the crown of poets. I have been your dupe for some time, and, whilst you showed a strong desire to visit Rome, I hoped to welcome you there. But my eyes are now opened to all your rogueries, which nevertheless, will not prevent me from loving you."

Petrarch, in his answer to the Bishop,[6] says, "My father, if I love the poets, I only follow, in this respect, the example of St. Augustine. I take the sainted father himself to witness the sincerity of my attachment to him. He is now in a place where he can neither deceive nor be deceived. I flatter myself that he pities my errors, especially when he recalls his own." St. Augustine had been somewhat profligate in his younger days.

"As to Laura," continues the poet, "would to Heaven that she were only an imaginary personage, and my passion for her only a pastime! Alas! it is a madness which it would be difficult and painful to feign for any length of time; and what an extravagance it would be to affect such a passion! One may counterfeit illness by action, by voice, and by manner, but no one in health can give himself the true air and complexion of disease. How often have you yourself been witness of my paleness and my sufferings! I know very well that you speak only in irony: it is your favourite figure of speech, but I hope that time will cicatrize these wounds of my spirit, and that Augustine, whom I pretend to love, will furnish me with a defence against a Laura who does not exist."

Years had now elapsed since Petrarch had conceived his passion for Laura; and it was obviously doomed to be a source of hopeless torment to him as long as he should continue near her; for she could breathe no more encouragement on his love than what was barely sufficient to keep it alive; and, if she had bestowed more favour on him, the consequences might have been ultimately most tragic to both of them. His own reflections, and the advice of his friends, suggested that absence and change of objects were the only means likely to lessen his misery; he determined, therefore, to travel once more, and set out for Rome in 1335.

The wish to assuage his passion, by means of absence, was his principal motive for going again upon his travels; but, before he could wind up his resolution to depart, the state of his mind bordered on distraction. One day he observed a country girl washing the veil of Laura; a sudden trembling seized him—and, though the heat of the weather was intense, he grew cold and shivered. For some time he was incapable of applying to study or business. His soul, he said, was like a field of battle, where his passion and reason held continual conflict. In his calmer moments, many agreeable motives for travelling suggested themselves to his mind. He had a strong desire to visit Rome, where he was sure of finding the kindest welcome from the Bishop of Lombes. He was to pass through Paris also; and there he had left some valued friends, to whom he had promised that he would return. At the head of those friends were Dionisio dal Borgo San Sepolcro and Roberto Bardi, a Florentine, whom the Pope had lately made chancellor of the Church of Paris, and given him the canonship of Nôtre Dame. Dionisio dal Borgo was a native of Tuscany, and one of the Roberti family. His name in literature was so considerable that Filippo Villani thought it worth while to write his life. Petrarch wrote his funeral eulogy, and alludes to Dionisio's power of reading futurity by the stars. But Petrarch had not a grain of faith in astrology; on the contrary, he has himself recorded that he derided it. After having obtained, with some difficulty, the permission of Cardinal Colonna, he took leave of his friends at Avignon, and set out for Marseilles. Embarking there in a ship that was setting sail for Civita Vecchia, he concealed his name, and gave himself out for a pilgrim going to worship at Rome. Great was his joy when, from the deck, he could discover the coast of his beloved Italy. It was a joy, nevertheless, chastened by one indomitable recollection—that of the idol he had left behind. On his landing he perceived a laurel tree; its name seemed to typify her who dwelt for ever in his heart: he flew to embrace it; but in his transports overlooked a brook that was between them, into which he fell—and the accident caused him to swoon. Always occupied with Laura, he says, "On those shores washed by the Tyrrhene sea, I beheld that stately laurel which always warms my imagination, and, through my impatience, fell breathless into the intervening stream. I was alone, and in the woods, yet I blushed at my own heedlessness; for, to the reflecting mind, no witness is necessary to excite the emotion of shame."

It was not easy for Petrarch to pass from the coast of Tuscany to Rome; for war between the Ursini and Colonna houses had been renewed with more fury than ever, and filled all the surrounding country with armed men. As he had no escort, he took refuge in the castle of Capranica, where he was hospitably received by Orso, Count of Anguillara, who had married Agnes Colonna, sister of the Cardinal and the Bishop. In his letter to the latter, Petrarch luxuriates in describing the romantic and rich landscape of Capranica, a country believed by the ancients to have been the first that was cultivated under the reign of Saturn. He draws, however, a frightful contrast to its rural picture in the horrors of war which here prevailed. "Peace," he says, "is the only charm which I could not find in this beautiful region. The shepherd, instead of guarding against wolves, goes armed into the woods to defend himself against men. The labourer, in a coat of mail, uses a lance instead of a goad, to drive his cattle. The fowler covers himself with a shield as he draws his nets; the fisherman carries a sword whilst he hooks his fish; and the native draws water from the well in an old rusty casque, instead of a pail. In a word, arms are used here as tools and implements for all the labours of the field, and all the wants of men. In the night are heard dreadful howlings round the walls of towns, and and in the day terrible voices crying incessantly to arms. What music is this compared with those soft and harmonious sounds which. I drew from my lute at Avignon!"

On his arrival at Capranica, Petrarch despatched a courier to the Bishop of Lombes, informing him where he was, and of his inability to get to Rome, all roads to it being beset by the enemy. The Bishop expressed great joy at his friend's arrival in Italy, and went to meet him at Capranica, with Stefano Colonna, his brother, senator of Rome. They had with them only a troop of one hundred horsemen; and, considering that the enemy kept possession of the country with five hundred men, it is wonderful that they met with no difficulties on their route; but the reputation of the Colonnas had struck terror into the hostile camp. They entered Rome without having had a single skirmish with the enemy. Stefano Colonna, in his quality of senator, occupied the Capitol, where he assigned apartments to Petrarch; and the poet was lodged on that famous hill which Scipio, Metellus, and Pompey, had ascended in triumph. Petrarch was received and treated by the Colonnas Like a child of their family. The venerable old Stefano, who had known him at Avignon, loaded our poet with kindness. But, of all the family, it would seem that Petrarch delighted most in the conversation of Giovanni da S. Vito, a younger brother of the aged Stefano, and uncle of the Cardinal and Bishop. Their tastes were congenial. Giovanni had made a particular study of the antiquities of Rome; he was, therefore, a most welcome cicerone to our poet, being, perhaps, the only Roman then alive, who understood the subject deeply, if we except Cola di Rienzo, of whom we shall soon have occasion to speak.

Castle of St. Angelo & St. Peters.

In company with Giovanni, Petrarch inspected the relics of the "eternal city:" the former was more versed than his companion in ancient history, but the other surpassed him in acquaintance with modern times, as well as with the objects of antiquity that stood immediately before them.

What an interesting object is Petrarch contemplating the ruins of Rome! He wrote to the Cardinal Colonna as follows:—"I gave you so long an account of Capranica that you may naturally expect a still longer description of Rome. My materials for this subject are, indeed, inexhaustible; but they will serve for some future opportunity. At present, I am so wonder-struck by so many great objects that I know not where to begin. One circumstance, however, I cannot omit, which has turned out contrary to your surmises. You represented to me that Rome was a city in ruins, and that it would not come up to the imagination I had formed of it; but this has not happened—on the contrary, my most sanguine expectations have been surpassed. Rome is greater, and her remains are more awful, than my imagination had conceived. It is not matter of wonder that she acquired universal dominion. I am only surprised that it was so late before she came to it."

In the midst of his meditations among the relics of Rome, Petrarch was struck by the ignorance about their forefathers, with which the natives looked on those monuments. The veneration which they had for them was vague and uninformed. "It is lamentable," he says, "that nowhere in the world is Rome less known than at Rome."

It is not exactly known in what month Petrarch left the Roman capital; but, between his departure from that city, and his return to the banks of the Rhone, he took an extensive tour over Europe. He made a voyage along its southern coasts, passed the straits of Gibraltar, and sailed as far northward as the British shores. During his wanderings, he wrote a letter to Tommaso da Messina, containing a long geographical dissertation on the island of Thule.

Petrarch approached the British shores; why were they not fated to have the honour of receiving him? Ah! but who was there, then, in England that was capable of receiving him? Chaucer was but a child. We had the names of some learned men, but our language had no literature. Time works wonders in a few centuries; and England, *now* proud of her Shakespeare and her Verulam, looks not with envy on the glory of any earthly nation. During his excitement by these travels, a singular change took place in our poet's habitual feelings. He recovered his health and spirits; he could bear to think of Laura with equanimity, and his countenance resumed the cheerfulness that was natural to a man in the strength of his age. Nay, he became so sanguine in his belief that he had overcome his passion as to jest at his past sufferings; and, in this gay state of mind, he came back to Avignon. This was the crowning misfortune of his life. He saw Laura once more; he was enthralled anew; and he might now laugh in agony at his late self-congratulations on his delivery from her enchantment. With all the pity that we bestow on unfortunate love, and with all the respect that we owe to its constancy, still we cannot look but with a regret amounting to impatience on a man returning to the spot that was to rekindle his passion as recklessly as a moth to the candle, and binding himself over for life to an affection that was worse than hopeless, inasmuch as its success would bring more misery than its failure. It is said that Petrarch, if it had not been for this passion, would not have been the poet that he was. Not, perhaps, so good an amatory poet; but I firmly believe that he would have been a more various and masculine, and, upon the whole, *a greater poet*, if he had never been bewitched by Laura. However, *he did* return to take possession of his canonicate at Lombes, and to lose possession of his peace of mind.

In the April of the following year, 1336, he made an excursion, in company with his brother Gherardo, to the top of Mount Ventoux, in the neighbourhood of Avignon; a full description of which he sent in a letter to Dionisio dal Borgo a San Sepolcro; but there is nothing peculiarly interesting in this occurrence.

A more important event in his life took place during the following year, 1337— namely, that he had a son born to him, whom he christened by the name of John, and to whom he acknowledged his relationship of paternity. With all his philosophy and platonic raptures about Laura, Petrarch was still subject to the passions of ordinary men, and had a mistress at Avignon who was kinder to him than Laura. Her name and history have been consigned to inscrutable obscurity: the same woman afterwards bore him a daughter, whose name was Francesca, and who proved a great solace to him in his old age. His biographers extol the magnanimity of Laura for displaying no anger at our poet for what they choose to call this discovery of his infidelity to her; but, as we have no reason to suppose that Laura ever bestowed one favour on Petrarch beyond a pleasant look, it is difficult to perceive her right to command his unspotted faith. At all events, she would have done no good to her own reputation if she had stormed at the lapse of her lover's virtue.

In a small city like Avignon, the scandal of his intrigue would naturally be a matter of regret to his friends and of triumph to his enemies. Petrarch felt his situation, and, unable to calm his mind either by the advice of his friend Dionisio dal Borgo, or by the perusal of his favourite author, St. Augustine, he resolved to seek a rural retreat, where he might at least hide his tears and his mortification. Unhappily he chose a spot not far enough from Laura—namely, Vaucluse, which is fifteen Italian, or about fourteen English, miles from Avignon.

Vaucluse, or Vallis Clausa, the shut-up valley, is a most beautiful spot, watered by the windings of the Sorgue. Along the river there are on one side most verdant plains and meadows, here and there shadowed by trees. On the other side are hills covered with corn and vineyards. Where the Sorgue rises, the view terminates in the cloud-capt ridges of the mountains Luberoux and Ventoux. This was the place which Petrarch had visited with such delight when he was a schoolboy, and at the sight of which he exclaimed "that he would prefer it as a residence to the most splendid city."

It is, indeed, one of the loveliest seclusions in the world. It terminates in a semicircle of rocks of stupendous height, that seem to have been hewn down perpendicularly. At the head and centre of the vast amphitheatre, and at the foot of one of its enormous rocks, there is a cavern of proportional size, hollowed out by the hand of nature. Its opening is an arch sixty feet high; but it is a double cavern, there being an interior one with an entrance thirty feet high. In the midst of these there is an oval basin, having eighteen fathoms for its longest diameter, and from this basin rises the copious stream which forms the Sorgue. The surface of the fountain is black, an appearance produced by its depth, from the darkness of the rocks, and the obscurity of the cavern; for, on being brought to light, nothing can be clearer than its water. Though beautiful to the eye, it is harsh to the taste, but is excellent for tanning and dyeing; and it is said to promote the growth of a plant which fattens oxen and is good for hens during incubation. Strabo and Pliny the naturalist both speak of its possessing this property.

The river Sorgue, which issues from this cavern, divides in its progress into various branches; it waters many parts of Provence, receives several tributary streams, and, after reuniting its branches, falls into the Rhone near Avignon.

Resolving to fix his residence here, Petrarch bought a little cottage and an adjoining field, and repaired to Vaucluse with no other companions than his books. To this day the ruins of a small house are shown at Vaucluse, which tradition says was his habitation.

Solitudes of Vaucluse.
"Fort de Bard", by James Duffield Harding (1797-1863)

If his object was to forget Laura, the composition of sonnets upon her in this hermitage was unlikely to be an antidote to his recollections. It would seem as if he meant to cherish rather than to get rid of his love. But, if he nursed his passion, it was a dry-nursing; for he led a lonely, ascetic, and, if it were not for his studies, we might say a savage life. In one of his letters, written not long after his settling at Vaucluse, he says, "Here I make war upon my senses, and treat them as my enemies. My eyes, which have drawn me into a thousand difficulties, see no longer either gold, or precious stones, or ivory, or purple; they behold nothing save the water, the firmament, and the rocks. The only female who comes within their sight is a swarthy old woman, dry and parched as the Lybian deserts. My ears are no longer courted by those harmonious instruments and voices which have so often transported my soul: they hear nothing but the lowing of cattle, the bleating of sheep, the warbling of birds, and the murmurs of the river.

"I keep silence from noon till night. There is no one to converse with; for the good people, employed in spreading their nets, or tending their vines and orchards, are no great adepts at conversation. I often content myself with the brown bread of the fisherman, and even eat it with pleasure. Nay, I almost prefer it to white bread. This old fisherman, who is as hard as iron, earnestly remonstrates against my manner of life; and assures me that I cannot long hold out. I am, on the contrary, convinced that it is easier to accustom one's self to a plain diet than to the luxuries of a feast. But still I have my luxuries—figs, raisins, nuts and almonds. I am fond of the fish with which this stream abounds, and I sometimes amuse myself with spreading the nets. As to my dress, there is an entire change; you would take me for a labourer or a shepherd.

"My mansion resembles that of Cato or Fabricius. My whole house-establishment consists of myself, my old fisherman and his wife, and a dog. My fisherman's cottage is contiguous to mine; when I want him I call; when I no longer need him, he returns to his cottage.

"I have made two gardens that please me wonderfully. I do not think they are to be equalled in all the world. And I must confess to you a more than female weakness with which I am haunted. I am positively angry that there is anything so beautiful out of Italy.

"One of these gardens is shady, formed for contemplation, and sacred to Apollo. It overhangs the source of the river, and is terminated by rocks, and by places accessible only to birds. The other is nearer my cottage, of an aspect less severe, and devoted to Bacchus; and what is extremely singular, it is in the midst of a rapid river. The approach to it is over a bridge of rocks; and there is a natural grotto under the rocks, which gives them the appearance of a rustic bridge. Into this grotto the rays of the sun never penetrate. I am confident that it much resembles the place where Cicero went to declaim. It invites to study. Hither I retreat during the noontide hours; my mornings are engaged upon the hills, or in the garden sacred to Apollo. Here I would most willingly pass my days, were I not too near Avignon, and too far from Italy. For why should I conceal this weakness of my soul? I love Italy, and I hate Avignon. The pestilential influence of this horrid place empoisons the pure air of Vaucluse, and will compel me to quit my retirement."

It is clear that he was not supremely contented in his solitude with his self-drawn mental resources. His friends at Avignon came seldom to see him. Travelling even short distances was difficult in those days. Even we, in the present day, can remember when the distance of fourteen miles presented a troublesome journey. The few guests who came, to him could not expect very exquisite dinners, cooked by the brown old woman and her husband the fisherman; and, though our poet had a garden consecrated to Bacchus, he had no cellar devoted to the same deity. His few friends, therefore, who visited him, thought their angel visits acts of charity. If he saw his friends seldom, however, he had frequent visitants in strangers who came to Vaucluse, as a place long celebrated for its natural beauties, and now made illustrious by the character and compositions of our poet. Among these there were persons distinguished for their rank or learning, who came from the farthest parts of France and from Italy, to see and converse with Petrarch. Some of them even sent before them considerable presents, which, though kindly meant, were not acceptable.

Vaucluse is in the diocese of Cavaillon, a small city about two miles distant from our poet's retreat. Philip de Cabassoles was the bishop, a man of high rank and noble family. His disposition, according to Petrarch's usual praise of his friends, was highly benevolent and humane; he was well versed in literature, and had distinguished abilities. No sooner was the poet settled in his retirement, than he visited the Bishop at his palace near Vaucluse. The latter gave him a friendly reception, and returned his visits frequently. Another much estimated, his friend since their childhood, Guido Sette, also repaired at times to his humble mansion, and relieved his solitude in the shut-up valley.[7]

Without some daily and constant occupation even the bright mind of Petrarch would have rusted, like the finest steel when it is left unscoured. But he continued his studies with an ardour that commands our wonder and respect; and it was at Vaucluse that he either meditated or wrote his most important compositions. Here he undertook a history of Rome, from Romulus down to Titus Vespasian. This Herculean task he never finished; but there remain two fragments of it, namely, four books, De Rebus Memorandis, and another tract entitled Vitarum Virorum Illustrium Epitome, being sketches of illustrious men from the founder of Rome down to Fabricius.

About his poem, Africa, I shall only say for the present that he began this Latin epic at Vaucluse, that its hero is his idolized Roman, Scipio Africanus, that it gained him a reputation over Europe, and that he was much pleased with it himself, but that his admiration of it in time cooled down so much, that at last he was annoyed when it was mentioned to him, and turned the conversation, if he could, to a different subject. Nay, it is probable, that if it had not been for Boccaccio and Coluccio Salutati, who, long after he had left Vaucluse, importuned him to finish and publish it, his Africa would not have come down to posterity.

Petrarch alludes in one of his letters to an excursion which he made in 1338, in company with a man whose rank was above his wisdom. He does not name him, but it seems clearly to have been Humbert II., Dauphin of the Viennois. The Cardinal Colonna forced our poet into this pilgrimage to Baume, famous for its adjacent cavern, where, according to the tradition of the country, Mary Magdalen passed thirty years of repentance. In that holy but horrible cavern, as Petrarch calls it, they remained three days and three nights, though Petrarch sometimes gave his comrades the slip, and indulged in rambles among the hills and forests; he composed a short poem, however, on St. Mary Magdalen, which is as dull as the cave itself. The Dauphin Humbert was not a bright man; but he seems to have contracted a friendly familiarity with our poet, if we may judge by a letter which Petrarch indited to him about this time, frankly reproaching him with his political neutrality in the affairs of Europe. It was supposed that the Cardinal Colonna incited him to write it. A struggle that was now impending between France and England engaged all Europe on one side or other. The Emperor Lewis had intimated to Humbert that he must follow him in this war, he, the Dauphin, being arch-seneschal of Arles and Vienne. Next year, the arch-seneschal received an invitation from Philip of Valois to join him with his troops at Amiens as vassal of France. The Dauphin tried to back out of the dilemma between his two suitors by frivolous excuses to both, all the time determining to assist neither. In 1338 he came to Avignon, and the Pope gave him his palace at the bridge of the Sorgue for his habitation. Here the poor craven, beset on one side by threatening letters from Philip of Valois, and on the other by importunities from the French party at the papal court, remained in Avignon till July, 1339, after Petrarch had let loose upon him his epistolary eloquence.

This letter, dated April, 1339, is, according to De Sade's opinion, full of powerful persuasion. I cannot say that it strikes me as such. After calling Christ to witness that he writes to the Dauphin in the spirit of friendship, he reminds him that Europe had never exhibited so mighty and interesting a war as that which had now sprung up between the kings of France and England, nor one that opened so vast a field of glory for the brave. "All the princes and their people," he says, "are anxious about its issue, especially those between the Alps and the ocean, who take arms at the crash of the neighbouring tumult; whilst you alone go to sleep amidst the clouds of the coming storm. To say the truth, if there was nothing more than shame to awaken you, it ought to rouse you from this lethargy. I had thought you," he continues, "a man desirous of glory. You are young and in the strength of life. What, then, in the name of God, keeps you inactive? Do you fear fatigue? Remember what Sallust says—'Idle enjoyments were made for women, fatigue was made for men.' Do you fear death? Death is the last debt we owe to nature, and man ought not to fear it; certainly he ought not to fear it more than sleep and sluggishness. Aristotle, it is true, calls death the last of horrible things; but, mind, he does not call it the most horrible of things." In this manner, our poet goes on moralizing on the blessings of an early death, and the great advantage that it would have afforded to some excellent Roman heroes if they had met with it sooner. The only thing like a sensible argument that he urges is, that Humbert could not expect to save himself even by neutrality, but must ultimately become the prey of the victor, and be punished like the Alban Metius, whom Tullus Hostilius caused to be torn asunder by horses that pulled his limbs in different directions. The pedantic epistle had no effect on Humbert.

Meanwhile, Italy had no repose more than the rest of Europe, but its troubles gave a happy occasion to Petrarch to see once more his friend, Guglielmo Pastrengo, who, in 1338, came to Avignon, from Mastino della Scala, lord of Verona.

The moment Petrarch heard of his friend's arrival he left his hermitage to welcome him; but scarcely had he reached the fatal city when he saw the danger of so near an approach to the woman he so madly loved, and was aware that he had no escape from the eyes of Laura but by flight. He returned, therefore, all of a sudden to Vaucluse, without waiting for a sight of Pastrengo. Shortly after he had quitted the house of Lælius, where he usually lodged when he went to Avignon, Guglielmo, expecting to find him there, knocked at the door, but no one opened it—called out, but no one answered him. He therefore wrote him a little billet, saying, "My dear Petrarch, where have you hid yourself, and whither have you vanished? What is the meaning of all this?" The poet received this note at Vaucluse, and sent an explanation of his flight, sincere indeed as to good feelings, but prolix as usual in the expression of them. Pastrengo sent him a kind reply, and soon afterwards did him the still greater favour of visiting him at Vaucluse, and helping him to cultivate his garden.

Petrarch's flame for Laura was in reality unabated. One day he met her in the streets of Avignon; for he had not always resolution enough to keep out of the western Babylon. Laura cast a kind look upon him, and said, "Petrarch, you are tired of loving me." This incident produced one of the finest sonnets, beginning—

Io non fut d' amar voi lassato unquanco.

> Tired, did you say, of loving you? Oh, no!
> I ne'er shall tire of the unwearying flame.
> But I am weary, kind and cruel dame,
> With tears that uselessly and ceaseless flow,
> Scorning myself, and scorn'd by you. I long
> For death: but let no gravestone hold in view
> Our names conjoin'd: nor tell my passion strong
> Upon the dust that glow'd through life for you.
> And yet this heart of amorous faith demands,
> Deserves, a better boon; but cruel, hard
> As is my fortune, I will bless Love's bands
> For ever, if you give me this reward.

In 1339, he composed among other sonnets, those three, the lxii., lxxiv., and lxxv., which are confessedly master-pieces of their kind, as well as three canzoni to the eyes of Laura, which the Italians call the three sister Graces, and worship as divine.[8] The critic Tassoni himself could not censure them, and called them the queens of song. At this period, however seldom he may have visited Avignon, he evidently sought rather to cherish than subdue his fatal attachment. A celebrated painter, Simone Martini of Siena, came to Avignon. He was the pupil of Giotto, not exquisite in drawing, but famous for taking spirited likenesses.

Petrarch persuaded Simone to favour him with a miniature likeness of Laura; and this treasure the poet for ever carried about with him. In gratitude he addressed two sonnets to the artist, whose fame, great as it was, was heightened by the poetical reward. Vasari tells us that Simone also painted the pictures of both lovers in the chapel of St. Maria Novella at Florence; that Simone was a sculptor as well as a painter, and that he copied those pictures in marbles which, according to Baldelli, are still extant in the house of the Signore Pruzzi.

An anecdote relating to this period of Petrarch's life is given by De Sade, which, if accepted with entire credence, must inspire us with astonishment at the poet's devotion to his literary pursuits. He had now, in 1339, put the first hand to his epic poem, the Scipiade; and one of his friends, De Sade believes that it was the Bishop of Lombes, fearing lest he might injure his health by overzealous application, went to ask him for the key of his library, which the poet gave up. The Bishop then locked up his books and papers, and commanded him to abstain from reading and writing for ten days. Petrarch obeyed; but on the first day of this literary Ramazan, he was seized with ennui, on the second with a severe headache, and on the third with symptoms of fever; the Bishop relented, and permitted the student to return to his books and papers.

Petrarch was at this time delighted, in his solitude of Vaucluse, to hear of the arrival at Avignon of one of his dearest friends. This was Dionisio dal Borgo a San Sepolcro, who, being now advanced in years, had resigned his pulpit in the University of Paris, in order to return to his native country, and came to Avignon with the intention of going by sea to Florence. Petrarch pressed him strongly to visit him at Vaucluse, interspersing his persuasion with many compliments to King Robert of Naples, to whom he knew that Dionisio was much attached; nor was he without hopes that his friend would speak favourably of him to his Neapolitan Majesty. In a letter from Vaucluse he says:—"Can nothing induce you to come to my solitude? Will not my ardent request, and the pity you must have for my condition, bring you to pass some days with your old disciple? If these motives are not sufficient, permit me to suggest another inducement. There is in this place a poplar-tree of so immense a size that it covers with its shade not only the river and its banks, but also a considerable extent beyond them. They tell us that King Robert of Naples, invited by the beauty of this spot, came hither to unburthen his mind from the weight of public affairs, and to enjoy himself in the shady retreat." The poet added many eulogies on his Majesty of Naples, which, as he anticipated, reached the royal ear. It seems not to be clear that Father Dionisio ever visited the poet at Vaucluse; though they certainly had an interview at Avignon. To Petrarch's misfortune, his friend's stay in that city was very short. The monk proceeded to Florence, but he found there no shady retreat like that of the poplar at Vaucluse. Florence was more than ever agitated by internal commotions, and was this year afflicted by plague and famine. This dismal state of the city determined Dionisio to accept an invitation from King Robert to spend the remainder of his days at his court.

This monarch had the happiness of giving additional publicity to Petrarch's reputation. That the poet sought his patronage need not be concealed; and if he used a little flattery in doing so, we must make allowance for the adulatory instinct of the tuneful tribe. We cannot live without bread upon bare reputation, or on the prospect of having tombstones put over our bones, prematurely hurried to the grave by hunger, when they shall be as insensible to praise as the stones themselves. To speak seriously, I think that a poet sacrifices his usefulness to himself and others, and an importance in society which may be turned to public good, if he shuns the patronage that can be obtained by unparasitical means.

Father Dionisio, upon his arrival at Naples, impressed the King with so favourable an opinion of Petrarch that Robert wrote a letter to our poet, enclosing an epitaph of his Majesty's own composition, on the death of his niece Clementina. This letter is unhappily lost; but the answer to it is preserved, in which Petrarch tells the monarch that his epitaph rendered his niece an object rather of envy than of lamentation. "O happy Clementina!" says the poet, "after passing through a transitory life, you have attained a double immortality, one in heaven, and another on earth." He then compares the posthumous good fortune of the princess to that of Achilles, who had been immortalized by Homer. It is possible that King Robert's letter to Petrarch was so laudatory as to require a flattering answer. But this reverberated praise is rather overstrained.

Petrarch was now intent on obtaining the honour of Poet Laureate. His wishes were at length gratified, and in a manner that made the offer more flattering than the crown itself.

Whilst he still remained at Vaucluse, at nine o'clock in the morning of the 1st of September, 1340, he received a letter from the Roman Senate, pressingly inviting him to come and receive the crown of Poet Laureate at Rome. He must have little notion of a poet's pride and vanity, who cannot imagine the flushed countenance, the dilated eyes, and the joyously-throbbing heart of Petrarch, whilst he read this letter. To be invited by the Senate of Rome to such an honour might excuse him for forgetting that Rome was not now what she had once been, and that the substantial glory of his appointment was small in comparison with the classic associations which formed its halo.

As if to keep up the fever of his joy, he received the same day, in the afternoon, at four o'clock, another letter with the same offer, from Roberto Bardi, Chancellor of the University of Paris, in which he importuned him to be crowned as Poet Laureate at Paris. When we consider the poet's veneration for Rome, we may easily anticipate that he would give the preference to that city. That he might not, however, offend his friend Roberto Bardi and the University of Paris, he despatched a messenger to Cardinal Colonna, asking his advice upon the subject, pretty well knowing that his patron's opinion would coincide with his own wishes. The Colonna advised him to be crowned at Rome.

The custom of conferring this honour had, for a long time, been obsolete. In the earliest classical ages, garlands were given as a reward to valour and genius. Virgil exhibits his conquerors adorned with them. The Romans adopted the custom from Greece, where leafy honours were bestowed on victors at public games. This coronation of poets, it is said, ceased under the reign of the Emperor Theodosius. After his death, during the long subsequent barbarism of Europe, when literature produced only rhyming monks, and when there were no more poets to crown, the discontinuance of the practice was a natural consequence.

At the commencement of the thirteenth century, according to the Abbé Resnel, the universities of Europe began to dispense laurels, not to poets, but to students distinguished by their learning. The doctors in medicine, at the famous university of Salerno, established by the Emperor Frederic II., had crowns of laurel put upon their heads. The bachelors also had their laurels, and derived their name from a baculus, or stick, which they carried.

Cardinal Colonna, as we have said, advised him, "*nothing loth*," to enjoy his coronation at Rome. Thither accordingly he repaired early in the year 1341. He embarked at Marseilles for Naples, wishing previously to his coronation to visit King Robert, by whom he was received with all possible hospitality and distinction.

Though he had accepted the laurel amidst the general applause of his contemporaries, Petrarch was not satisfied that he should enjoy this honour without passing through an ordeal as to his learning, for laurels and learning had been for one hundred years habitually associated in men's minds. The person whom Petrarch selected for his examiner in erudition was the King of Naples. Robert *the Good*, as he was in some respects deservedly called, was, for his age, a well-instructed man, and, for a king, a prodigy. He had also some common sense, but in classical knowledge he was more fit to be the scholar of Petrarch than his examiner. If Petrarch, however, learned nothing from the King, the King learned something from Petrarch. Among the other requisites for examining a Poet Laureate which Robert possessed, was *an utter ignorance of poetry*. But Petrarch couched his blindness on the subject, so that Robert saw, or believed he saw, something useful in the divine art. He had heard of the epic poem, Africa, and requested its author to recite to him some part of it. The King was charmed with the recitation, and requested that the work might be dedicated to him. Petrarch assented, but the poem was not finished or published till after King Robert's death.

His Neapolitan Majesty, after pronouncing a warm eulogy on our poet, declared that he merited the laurel, and had letters patent drawn up, by which he certified that, after a *severe* examination (it lasted three days), Petrarch was judged worthy to receive that honour in the Capitol. Robert wished him to be crowned at Naples; but our poet represented that he was desirous of being distinguished on the same theatre where Virgil and Horace had shone. The King accorded with his wishes; and, to complete his kindness, regretted that his advanced age would not permit him to go to Rome, and crown Petrarch himself. He named, however, one of his most eminent courtiers, Barrilli, to be his proxy. Boccaccio speaks of Barrilli as a good poet; and Petrarch, with exaggerated politeness, compares him to Ovid.

When Petrarch went to take leave of King Robert, the sovereign, after engaging his promise that he would visit him again very soon, took off the robe which he wore that day, and, begging Petrarch's acceptance of it, desired that he might wear it on the day of his coronation. He also bestowed on him the place of his almoner-general, an office for which great interest was always made, on account of the privileges attached to it, the principal of which were an exemption from paying the tithes of benefices to the King, and a dispensation from residence.

Petrarch proceeded to Rome, where he arrived on the 6th of April, 1341, accompanied by only one attendant from the court of Naples, for Barrilli had taken another route, upon some important business, promising, however, to be at Rome before the time appointed. But as he had not arrived on the 7th, Petrarch despatched a messenger in search of him, who returned without any information. The poet was desirous to wait for his arrival; but Orso, Count of Anguillara, would not suffer the ceremony to be deferred. Orso was joint senator of Rome with Giordano degli Orsini; and, his office expiring on the 8th of April, he was unwilling to resign to his successor the pleasure of crowning so great a man.

Naples.

Petrarch was afterwards informed that Barrilli, hastening towards Rome, had been beset near Anaguia by robbers, from whom he escaped with difficulty, and that he was obliged for safety to return to Naples. In leaving that city, Petrarch passed the tomb traditionally said to be that of Virgil. His coronation took place without delay after his arrival at Rome.

The morning of the 8th of April, 1341, was ushered in by the sound of trumpets; and the people, ever fond of a show, came from all quarters to see the ceremony. Twelve youths selected from the best families of Rome, and clothed in scarlet, opened the procession, repeating as they went some verses, composed by the poet, in honour of the Roman people. They were followed by six citizens of Rome, clothed in green, and bearing crowns wreathed with different flowers. Petrarch walked in the midst of them; after him came the senator, accompanied by the first men of the council. The streets were strewed with flowers, and the windows filled with ladies, dressed in the most splendid manner, who showered perfumed waters profusely on the poet[9]. He all the time wore the robe that had been presented to him by the King of Naples. When they reached the Capitol, the trumpets were silent, and Petrarch, having made a short speech, in which he quoted a verse from Virgil, cried out three times, "Long live the Roman people! long live the Senators! may God preserve their liberty!" At the conclusion of these words, he knelt before the senator Orso, who, taking a crown of laurel from his own head, placed it on that of Petrarch, saying, "This crown is the reward of virtue." The poet then repeated a sonnet in praise of the ancient Romans. The people testified their approbation by shouts of applause, crying, "Long flourish the Capitol and the poet!" The friends of Petrarch shed tears of joy, and Stefano Colonna, his favourite hero, addressed the assembly in his honour.

The ceremony having been finished at the Capitol, the procession, amidst the sound of trumpets and the acclamations of the people, repaired thence to the church of St. Peter, where Petrarch offered up his crown of laurel before the altar. The same day the Count of Anguillara caused letters patent to be delivered to Petrarch, in which the senators, after a flattering preamble, declared that he had merited the title of a great poet and historian; that, to mark his distinction, they had put upon his head a laurel crown, not only by the authority of Kong Robert, but by that of the Roman Senate and people; and that they gave him, at Rome and elsewhere, the privilege to read, to dispute, to explain ancient books, to make new ones, to compose poems, and to wear a crown according to his choice, either of laurel, beech, or myrtle, as well as the poetic habit. At that time a particular dress was affected by the poets. Dante was buried in this costume.

Petrarch continued only a few days at Rome after his coronation; but he had scarcely departed when he found that there were banditti on the road waiting for him, and anxious to relieve him of any superfluous wealth which he might have about him. He was thus obliged to return to Rome with all expedition; but he set out the following day, attended by a guard of armed men, and arrived at Pisa on the 20th of April.

From Pisa he went to Parma, to see his friend Azzo Correggio, and soon after his arrival he was witness to a revolution in that city of which Azzo had the principal direction. The Scalas, who held the sovereignty of Parma, had for some time oppressed the inhabitants with exorbitant taxes, which excited murmurs and seditions. The Correggios, to whom the city was entrusted in the absence of Mastino della Scala, profited by the public discontent, hoisted the flag of liberty, and, on the 22nd of May, 1341, drove out the garrison, and made themselves lords of the commonwealth. On this occasion, Azzo has been accused of the worst ingratitude to his nephews, Alberto and Mastino. But, if the people were oppressed, he was surely justified in rescuing them from misgovernment. To a great degree, also, the conduct of the Correggios sanctioned the revolution. They introduced into Parma such a mild and equitable administration as the city had never before experienced. Some exceptionable acts they undoubtedly committed; and when Petrarch extols Azzo as another Cato, it is to be hoped that he did so with some mental reservation. Petrarch had proposed to cross the Alps immediately, and proceed to Avignon; but he was prevailed upon by the solicitations of Azzo to remain some time at Parma. He was consulted by the Correggios on their most important affairs, and was admitted to their secret councils. In the present instance, this confidence was peculiarly agreeable to him; as the four brothers were, at that time, unanimous in their opinions; and their designs were all calculated to promote the welfare of their subjects.

Soon after his arrival at Parma, he received one of those tokens, of his popularity which are exceedingly expressive, though they come from a humble admirer. A blind old man, who had been a grammar-school master at Pontremoli, came to Parma, in order to pay his devotions to the laureate. The poor man had already walked to Naples, guided in his blindness by his only son, for the purpose of finding Petrarch. The poet had left that city; but King Robert, pleased with his enthusiasm, made him a present of some money. The aged pilgrim returned to Pontremoti, where, being informed that Petrarch was at Parma, he crossed the Apennines, in spite of the severity of the weather, and travelled thither, having sent before him a tolerable copy of verses. He was presented to Petrarch, whose hand he kissed with devotion and exclamations of joy. One day, before many spectators, the blind man said to Petrarch, "Sir, I have come far to see you." The bystanders laughed, on which the old man replied, "I appeal to you, Petrarch, whether I do not see you more clearly and distinctly than these men who have their eyesight." Petrarch gave him a kind reception, and dismissed him with a considerable present.

The pleasure which Petrarch had in retirement, reading, and reflection, induced him to hire a house on the outskirts of the city of Parma, with a garden, beautifully watered by a stream, a *rus in urbe*, as he calls it; and he was so pleased with this locality, that he purchased and embellished it.

Selva Piana, near Parma.

His happiness, however, he tells us, was here embittered by the loss of some friends who shared the first place in his affections. One of these was Tommaso da Messina, with whom he had formed a friendship when they were fellow-students at Bologna, and ever since kept up a familiar correspondence. They were of the same age, addicted to the same pursuits, and imbued with similar sentiments. Tommaso wrote a volume of Latin poems, several of which were published after the invention of printing. Petrarch, in his Triumphs of Love, reckons him an excellent poet.

This loss was followed by another which affected Petrarch still more strongly. Having received frequent invitations to Lombes from the Bishop, who had resided some time in his diocese, Petrarch looked forward with pleasure to the time when he should revisit him. But he received accounts that the Bishop was taken dangerously ill. Whilst his mind was agitated by this news, he had the following dream, which he has himself related. "Methought I saw the Bishop crossing the rivulet of my garden alone. I was astonished at this meeting, and asked him whence he came, whither he was going in such haste, and why he was alone. He smiled upon me with his usual complacency, and said, 'Remember that when you were in Gascony the tempestuous climate was insupportable to you. I also am tired of it. I have quitted Gascony, never to return, and I am going to Rome.' At the conclusion of these words, he had reached the end of the garden, and, as I endeavoured to accompany him, he in the kindest and gentlest manner waved his hand; but, upon my persevering, he cried out in a more peremptory manner, 'Stay! you must not at present attend me.' Whilst he spoke these words, I fixed my eyes upon him, and saw the paleness of death upon his countenance. Seized with horror, I uttered a loud cry, which awoke me. I took notice of the time. I told the circumstance to all my friends; and, at the expiration of five-and-twenty days, I received accounts of his death, which happened in the very same night in winch he had appeared to me."

On a little reflection, this incident will not appear to be supernatural. That Petrarch, oppressed as he was with anxiety about his friend, should fall into fanciful reveries during his sleep, and imagine that he saw him in the paleness of death, was nothing wonderful—nay, that he should frame this allegory in his dream is equally conceivable. The sleeper's imagination is often a great improvisatore. It forms scenes and stories; it puts questions, and answers them itself, all the time believing that the responses come from those whom it interrogates.

Petrarch, deeply attached to Azzo da Correggio, now began to consider himself as settled at Parma, where he enjoyed literary retirement in the bosom of his beloved Italy. But he had not resided there a year, when he was summoned to Avignon by orders he considered that he could not disobey. Tiraboschi, and after him Baldelli, ascribe his return to Avignon to the commission which he received in 1342, to go as advocate of the Roman people to the new Pope, Clement VI., who had succeeded to the tiara on the death of Benedict XII., and Petrarch's own words coincide with what they say. The feelings of joy with which Petrarch revisited Avignon, though to appearance he had weaned himself from Laura, may be imagined. He had friendship, however, if he had not love, to welcome him. Here he met, with reciprocal gladness, his friends Socrates and Lælius, who had established themselves at the court of the Cardinal Colonna. "Socrates," says De Sade, "devoted himself entirely to Petrarch, and even went with him to Vaucluse." It thus appears that Petrarch had not given up his peculium on the Sorgue, nor had any one rented the field and cottage in his absence.

Benedict's successor, Clement VI., was conversant with the world, and accustomed to the splendour of courts. Quite a contrast to the plain rigidity of Benedict, he was courteous and munificent, but withal a voluptuary; and his luxury and profusion gave rise to extortions, to rapine, and to boundless simony. His artful and arrogant mistress, the Countess of Turenne, ruled him so absolutely, that all places in his gift, which had escaped the grasp of his relations, were disposed of through her interest; and she amassed great wealth by the sale of benefices.

The Romans applied to Clement VI., as they had applied to Benedict XII., imploring him to bring back the sacred seat to their capital; and they selected Petrarch to be among those who should present their supplication. Our poet appealed to his Holiness on this subject, both in prose and verse. The Pope received him with smiles, complimented him on his eloquence, bestowed on him the priory of Migliorino, but, for the present, consigned his remonstrance to oblivion.

In this mission to Clement at Avignon there was joined with Petrarch the famous Nicola Gabrino, better known by the name Cola di Rienzo, who, very soon afterwards, attached the history of Rome to his biography. He was for the present comparatively little known; but Petrarch, thus coming into connection with this extraordinary person, was captivated with his eloquence, whilst Clement complimented Rienzo, admitted him daily to his presence, and conversed with him on the wretched state of Rome, the tyranny of the nobles, and the sufferings of the people.

Cola and Petrarch were the two chiefs of this Roman embassy to the Pope; and it appears that the poet gave precedency to the future tribune on this occasion. They both elaborately exposed the three demands of the Roman people, namely, that the Pope, already the acknowledged patron of Rome, should assume the title and functions of its senator, in order to extinguish the civil wars kindled by the Roman barons; that he should return to his pontifical chair on the banks of the Tiber; and that he should grant permission for the jubilee, instituted by Boniface VIII., to be held every fifty years, and not at the end of a century, as its extension to the latter period went far beyond the ordinary duration of human life, and cut off the greater part of the faithful from enjoying the institution.

Clement praised both orators, and conceded that the Romans should have a jubilee every fifty years; but he excused himself from going to Rome, alleging that he was prevented by the disputes between France and England. "Holy Father," said Petrarch, "how much it were to be wished that you had known Italy before you knew France." "I wish I had," said the Pontiff, very coldly.

Petrarch gave vent to his indignation at the papal court in a writing, entitled, "A Book of Letters without a Title," and in several severe sonnets. The "Liber Epistolarum sine Titulo" contains, as it is printed in his works (Basle edit., 1581), eighteen letters, fulminating as freely against papal luxury and corruption as if they had been penned by Luther or John Knox. From their contents, we might set down Petrarch as the earliest preacher of the Reformation, if there were not, in the writings of Dante, some passages of the same stamp. If these epistles were really circulated at the time when they were written, it is matter of astonishment that Petrarch never suffered from any other flames than those of love; for many honest reformers, who have been roasted alive, have uttered less anti-papal vituperation than our poet; nor, although Petrarch would have been startled at a revolution in the hierarchy, can it be doubted that his writings contributed to the Reformation.

It must be remembered, at the same time, that he wrote against the church government of Avignon, and not that of Rome. He compares Avignon with the Assyrian Babylon, with Egypt under the mad tyranny of Cambyses; or rather, denies that the latter empires can be held as parallels of guilt to the western Babylon; nay, he tells us that neither Avernus nor Tartarus can be confronted with this infernal place.

"The successors of a troop of fishermen," he says, "have forgotten their origin. They are not contented, like the first followers of Christ, who gained their livelihood by the Lake of Gennesareth, with modest habitations, but they must build themselves splendid palaces, and go about covered with gold and purple. They are fishers of men, who catch a credulous multitude, and devour them for their prey." This "Liber Epistolarum" includes some descriptions of the debaucheries of the churchmen, which are too scandalous for translation. They are nevertheless curious relics of history.

In this year, Gherardo, the brother of our poet, retired, by his advice, to the Carthusian monastery of Montrieux, which they had both visited in the pilgrimage to Baume three years before. Gherardo had been struck down with affliction by the death of a beautiful woman at Avignon, to whom he was devoted. Her name and history are quite unknown, but it may be hoped, if not conjectured, that she was not married, and could be more liberal in her affections than the poet's Laura.

Amidst all the incidents of this period of his life, the attachment of Petrarch to Laura continued unabated. It appears, too, that, since his return from Parma, she treated him with more than wonted complacency. He passed the greater part of the year 1342 at Avignon, and went to Vaucluse but seldom and for short intervals.

In the meantime, love, that makes other people idle, interfered not with Petrarch's fondness for study. He found an opportunity of commencing the study of Greek, and seized it with avidity. That language had never been totally extinct in Italy; but at the time on which we are touching, there were not probably six persons in the whole country acquainted with it. Dante had quoted Greek authors, but without having known the Greek alphabet. The person who favoured Petrarch with this coveted instruction was Bernardo Barlaamo, a Calabrian monk, who had been three years before at Avignon, having come as envoy from Andronicus, the eastern Emperor, on pretext of proposing a union between the Greek and Roman churches, but, in reality for the purpose of trying to borrow money from the Pope for the

Emperor. Some of Petrarch's biographers date his commencement of the study of Greek from the period of Barlaamo's first visit to Avignon; but I am inclined to postpone it to 1342, when Barlaamo returned to the west and settled at Avignon. Petrarch began studying Greek by the reading of Plato. He never obtained instruction sufficient to make him a good Grecian, but he imbibed much of the spirit of Plato from the labour which he bestowed on his works. He was very anxious to continue his Greek readings with Barlaamo; but his stay in Avignon was very short; and, though it was his interest to detain him as his preceptor, Petrarch, finding that he was anxious for a settlement in Italy, helped him to obtain the bishopric of Geraci, in Calabria.

Nice, Coast of Genoa. Artist: James Duffield Harding (1797-1863).

The next year was memorable in our poet's life for the birth of his daughter Francesca. That the mother of this daughter was the same who presented him with his son John there can be no doubt. Baldelli discovers, in one of Petrarch's letters, an obscure allusion to her, which seems to indicate that she died suddenly after the birth of Francesca, who proved a comfort to her father in his old age.

The opening of the year 1343 brought a new loss to Petrarch in the death of Robert, King of Naples. Petrarch, as we have seen, had occasion to be grateful to this monarch; and we need not doubt that he was much affected by the news of his death; but, when we are told that he repaired to Vaucluse to bewail his irreparable loss, we may suppose, without uncharitableness, that he retired also with a view to study the expression of his grief no less than to cherish it. He wrote, however, an interesting letter on the occasion to Barbato di Sulmona, in which he very sensibly exhibits his fears of the calamities which were likely to result from the death of Robert, adding that his mind was seldom true in prophecy, unless when it foreboded misfortunes; and his predictions on this occasion were but too well verified.

Robert was succeeded by his granddaughter Giovanna, a girl of sixteen, already married to Andrew of Hungary, her cousin, who was but a few months older. Robert by his will had established a council of regency, which was to continue until Giovanna arrived at the age of twenty-five. The Pope, however, made objections to this arrangement, alleging that the administration of affairs during the Queen's minority devolved upon him immediately as lord superior. But, as he did not choose to assert his right till he should receive more accurate information respecting the state of the kingdom, he gave Petrarch a commission for that purpose; and entrusted him with a negotiation of much importance and delicacy.

Petrarch received an additional commission from the Cardinal Colonna. Several friends of the Colonna family were, at that time, confined in prison at Naples, and the Cardinal flattered himself that Petrarch's eloquence and intercession would obtain their enlargement. Our poet accepted the embassy. He went to Nice, where he embarked; but had nearly been lost in his passage. He wrote to Cardinal Colonna the following account of his voyage.

"I embarked at Nice, the first maritime town in Italy (he means the nearest to France). At night I got to Monaco, and the bad weather obliged me to pass a whole day there, which by no means put me into good-humour. The next morning we re-embarked, and, after being tossed all day by the tempest, we arrived very late at Port Maurice. The night was dreadful; it was impossible to get to the castle, and I was obliged to put up at a little village, where my bed and supper appeared tolerable from extreme weariness. I determined to proceed by land; the perils of the road appeared less dreadful to me than those by sea. I left my servants and baggage in the ship, which set sail, and I remained with only one domestic on shore. By accident, upon the coast of Genoa, I found some German horses which were for sale; they were strong and serviceable. I bought them; but I was soon afterwards obliged to take ship again; for war was renewed between the Pisans and the Milanese. Nature has placed limits to these States, the Po on one side, and the Apennines on the other. I must have passed between their two armies if I had gone by land; this obliged me to re-embark at Lerici. I passed by Corvo, that famous rock, the ruins of the city of Luna, and landed at Murrona. Thence I went the next day on horseback to Pisa, Siena, and Rome. My eagerness to execute your orders has made me a night-traveller, contrary to my character and disposition. I would not sleep till I had paid my duty to your illustrious father, who is always my hero. I found him the same as I left him seven years ago, nay, even as hale and sprightly as when I saw him at Avignon, which is now twelve years. What a surprising man! What strength of mind and body! How firm his voice! How beautiful his face! Had he been a few years younger, I should have taken him for Julius Cæsar, or Scipio Africanus. Rome grows old; but not its hero. He was half undressed, and going to bed; so I stayed only a moment, but I passed the whole of the next day with him. He asked me a thousand questions about you, and was much pleased that I was going to Naples. When I set out from Rome, he insisted on accompanying me beyond the walls.

"I reached Palestrina that night, and was kindly received by your nephew John. He is a young man of great hopes, and follows the steps of his ancestors.

"I arrived at Naples the 11th of October. Heavens, what a change has the death of one man produced in that place! No one would know it now. Religion, Justice, and Truth are banished. I think I am at Memphis, Babylon, or Mecca. In the stead of a king so just and so pious, a little monk, fat, rosy, barefooted, with a shorn head, and half covered with a dirty mantle, bent by hypocrisy more than by age, lost in debauchery whilst proud of his affected poverty, and still more of the real wealth he has amassed—this man holds the reins of this staggering empire. In vice and cruelty he rivals a Dionysius, an Agathocles, or a Phalaris. This monk, named Roberto, was an Hungarian cordelier, and preceptor of Prince Andrew, whom he entirely sways. He oppresses the weak, despises the great, tramples justice under foot, and treats both the dowager and the reigning Queen with the greatest insolence. The court and city tremble before him; a mournful silence reigns in the public assemblies, and in private they converse by whispers. The least gesture is punished, and *to think* is denounced as a crime. To this man I have presented the orders of the Sovereign Pontiff, and your just demands. He behaved with incredible insolence. Susa, or Damascus, the capital of the Saracens, would have received with more respect an envoy from the Holy See. The great lords imitate his pride and tyranny. The Bishop of Cavaillon is the only one who opposes this torrent; but what can one lamb do in the midst of so many wolves? It is the request of a dying king alone that makes him endure so wretched a situation. How small are the hopes of my negotiation! but I shall wait with patience; though I know beforehand the answer they will give me."

It is plain from Petrarch's letter that the kingdom of Naples was now under a miserable subjection to the Hungarian faction, aid that the young Queen's situation was anything but enviable. Few characters in modern history have been drawn in such contrasted colours as that of Giovanna, Queen of Naples. She has been charged with every vice, and extolled for every virtue. Petrarch represents her as a woman of weak understanding, disposed to gallantry, but incapable of greater crimes. Her history reminds us much of that of Mary Queen of Scots. Her youth and her character, gentle and interesting in several respects, entitle her to the benefit of our doubts as to her assent to the death of Andrew. Many circumstances seem to me to favour those doubts, and the opinion of Petrarch is on the side of her acquittal.

On his arrival in Naples, Petrarch had an audience with the Queen Dowager; but her grief and tears for the loss of her husband made this interview brief and fruitless with regard to business. When he spoke to her about the prisoners, for whose release the Colonnas had desired him to intercede, her Majesty referred him to the council. She was now, in reality, only a state cypher.

The principal prisoners for whom Petrarch was commissioned to plead, were the Counts Minervino, di Lucera, and Pontenza. Petrarch applied to the council of state in their behalf, but he was put off with perpetual excuses. While the affair was in agitation he went to Capua, where the prisoners were confined. "There," he writes to the Cardinal Colonna, "I saw your friends; and, such is the instability of Fortune, that I found them in chains. They support their situation with fortitude. Their innocence is no plea in their behalf to those who have shared in the spoils of their fortune. Their only expectations rest upon you. I have no hopes, except from the intervention of some superior power, as any dependence on the clemency of the council is out of the question. The Queen Dowager, now the most desolate of widows, compassionates their case, but cannot assist them."

Petrarch, wearied with the delays of business, sought relief in excursions to the neighbourhood. Of these he writes an account to Cardinal Colonna.

"I went to Baiæ," he says, "with my friends, Barbato and Barrilli. Everything concurred to render this jaunt agreeable—good company, the beauty of the scenes, and my extreme weariness of the city I had quitted. This climate, which, as far as I can judge, must be insupportable in summer, is delightful in winter. I was rejoiced to behold places described by Virgil, and, what is more surprising, by Homer before him. I have seen the Lucrine lake, famous for its fine oysters; the lake Avernus, with water as black as pitch, and fishes of the same colour swimming in it; marshes formed by the standing waters of Acheron, and the mountain whose roots go down to hell. The terrible aspect of this place, the thick shades with which it is covered by a surrounding wood, and the pestilent odour which this water exhales, characterize it very justly as the Tartarus of the poets. There wants only the boat of Charon, which, however, would be unnecessary, as there is only a shallow ford to pass over. The Styx and the kingdom of Pluto are now hid from our sight. Awed by what I had heard and read of these mournful approaches to the dead, I was contented to view them at my feet from the top of a high mountain. The labourer, the shepherd, and the sailor, dare not approach them nearer. There are deep caverns, where some pretend that a great deal of gold is concealed; covetous men, they say, have been to seek it, but they never return; whether they lost their way in the dark valleys, or had a fancy to visit the dead, being so near their habitations.

"I have seen the ruins of the grotto of the famous Cumæan sybil; it is a hideous rock, suspended in the Avernian lake. Its situation strikes the mind with horror. There still remain the hundred mouths by which the gods conveyed their oracles; these are now dumb, and there is only one God who speaks in heaven and on earth. These uninhabited ruins serve as the resort of birds of unlucky omen. Not far off is that dreadful cavern which leads, *they say*, to the infernal regions. Who would believe that, close to the mansions of the dead, Nature should have placed powerful remedies for the preservation of life? Near Avernus and Acheron are situated that barren land whence rises continually a salutary vapour, which is a cure for several diseases, and those hot-springs that vomit hot and sulphureous cinders. I have seen the baths which Nature has prepared; but the avarice of physicians has rendered them of doubtful use. This does not, however, prevent them from being visited by the invalids of all the neighbouring towns. These hollowed mountains dazzle us with the lustre of their marble circles, on which are engraved figures that point out, by the position of their hands, the part of the body which each fountain is proper to cure.

"I saw the foundations of that admirable reservoir of Nero, which was to go from Mount Misenus to the Avernian lake, and to enclose all the hot waters of Baiæ.

"At Pozzuoli I saw the mountain of Falernus, celebrated for its grapes, whence the famous Falernian wine. I saw likewise those enraged waves of which Virgil speaks in his Georgics, on which Cæsar put a bridle by the mole which he raised there, and which Augustus finished. It is now called the Dead Sea. I am surprised at the prodigious expense the Romans were at to build houses in the most exposed situations, in order to shelter them from the severities of the weather; for in the heats of summer the valleys of the Apennines, the mountains of Viterbo, and the woods of Umbria, furnished them with charming shades; and even the ruins of the houses which they built in those places are superb."

Our poet's residence at Naples was evidently disagreeable to him, in spite of the company of his friends, Barrilli and Barbato. His friendship with the latter was for a moment overcast by an act of indiscretion on the part of Barbato, who, by dint of importunity, obtained from Petrarch thirty-four lines of his poem of Africa, under a promise that he would show them to nobody. On entering the library of another friend, the first thing that struck our poet's eyes was a copy of the same verses, transcribed with a good many blunders. Petrarch's vanity on this occasion, however, was touched more than his anger—he forgave his friend's treachery, believing it to have arisen from excessive admiration. Barbato, as some atonement, gave him a little

MS. of Cicero, which Petrarch found to contain two books of the orator's Treatise on the Academics, "a work," as he observes, "more subtle than useful."

Queen Giovanna was fond of literature. She had several conversations with Petrarch, which increased her admiration of him. After the example of her grandfather, she made him her chaplain and household clerk, both of which offices must be supposed to have been sinecures. Her letters appointing him to them are dated the 25th of November, 1343, the very day before that nocturnal storm of which I shall speedily quote the poet's description.

Voltaire has asserted that the young Queen of Naples was the pupil of Petrarch; "but of this," as De Sade remarks, "there is no proof." It only appears that the two greatest geniuses of Italy, Boccaccio and Petrarch, were both attached to Giovanna, and had a more charitable opinion of her than most of their contemporaries.

Soon after his return from the tour to Baiæ, Petrarch was witness to a violent tempest at Naples, which most historians have mentioned, as it was memorable for having threatened the entire destruction of the city.

The night of the 25th of November, 1343, set in with uncommonly still weather; but suddenly a tempest rose violently in the direction of the sea, which made the buildings of the city shake to their very foundations. "At the first onset of the tempest," Petrarch writes to the Cardinal Colonna, "the windows of the house were burst open. The lamp of my chamber"—he was lodged at a monastery—"was blown out—I was shaken from my bed with violence, and I apprehended immediate death. The friars and prior of the convent, who had risen to pay their customary devotions, rushed into my room with crucifixes and relics in their hands, imploring the mercy of the Deity. I took courage, and accompanied them to the church, where we all passed the night, expecting every moment to be our last. I cannot describe the horrors of that dreadful night; the bursts of lightning and the roaring of thunder were blended with the shrieks of the people. The night itself appeared protracted to an unnatural length; and, when the morning arrived, which we discovered rather by conjecture than by any dawning of light, the priests prepared to celebrate the service; but the rest of us, not having yet dared to lift up our eyes towards the heavens, threw ourselves prostrate on the ground. At length the day appeared—a day how like to night! The cries of the people began to cease in the upper part of the city, but were redoubled from the sea-shore. Despair inspired us with courage. We mounted our horses and arrived at the port. What a scene was there! the vessels had suffered shipwreck in the very harbour; the shore was covered with dead bodies, which were tossed about and dashed against the rocks, whilst many appeared struggling in the agonies of death. Meanwhile, the raging ocean overturned many houses from their very foundations. Above a thousand Neapolitan horsemen were assembled near the shore to assist, as it were, at the obsequies of their countrymen. I caught from them a spirit of resolution, and was less afraid of death from the consideration that we should all perish together. On a sudden a cry of horror was heard; the sea had sapped the foundations of the ground on which we stood, and it was already beginning to give way. We immediately hastened to a higher place, where the scene was equally impressive. The young Queen, with naked feet and dishevelled hair, attended by a number of women, was rushing to the church of the Virgin, crying out for mercy in this imminent peril. At sea, no ship escaped the fury of the tempest: all the vessels in the harbour—one only excepted—sunk before our eyes, and every soul on board perished."

By the assiduity and solicitations of Petrarch, the council of Naples were at last engaged in debating about the liberation of Colonna's imprisoned friends; and the affair was nearly brought to a conclusion, when the approach of night obliged the members to separate before they came to a final decision. The cause of this separation is a sad proof of Neapolitan barbarism at that period. It will hardly, at this day, seem credible that, in the capital of so flourishing a kingdom, and the residence of a brilliant court, such savage licentiousness could have prevailed. At night, all the streets of the city were beset by the young nobility, who were armed, and who attacked all passengers without distinction, so that even the members of the council could not venture to appear after a certain hour. Neither the severity of parents, nor the authority of the magistrates, nor of Majesty itself, could prevent continual combats and assassinations.

"But can it be astonishing," Petrarch remarks, "that such disgraceful scenes should pass in the night, when the Neapolitans celebrate, even in the face of day, games similar to those of the gladiators, and with more than barbarian cruelty? Human blood is shed here with as little remorse as that of brute animals; and, while the people join madly in applause, sons expire in the very sight of their parents; and it is considered the utmost disgrace not to die with becoming fortitude, as if they were dying in the defence of their religion and country. I myself, ignorant of these customs was once carried to the Carbonara, the destined place of butchery. The Queen and her husband, Andrew, were present; the soldiery of Naples were present, and the people flocked thither in crowds. I was kept in suspense by the appearance of so large and brilliant an assembly, and expected some spectacle worthy of my attention, when I suddenly heard a loud shout of applause, as for some joyous incident. What was my surprise when I beheld a beautiful young man pierced through with a sword, and ready to expire at my feet! Struck with horror, I put spurs to my horse, and fled from the barbarous sight, uttering execrations on the cruel spectators.

"This inhuman custom has been derived from their ancestors, and is now so sanctioned by inveterate habit, that their very licentiousness is dignified with the name of liberty.

"You will cease to wonder at the imprisonment of your friends in this city, where the death of a young man is considered as an innocent pastime. As to myself, I will quit this inhuman country before three days are past, and hasten to you who can make all things agreeable to me except a sea-voyage."

Petrarch at length brought his negotiations respecting the prisoners to a successful issue; and they were released by the express authority of Andrew. Our poet's presence being no longer necessary, he left Naples, in spite of the strong solicitations of his friends Barrilli and Barbato. In answer to their request that he would remain, he said, "I am but a satellite, and follow the directions of a superior planet; quiet and repose are denied to me."

From Naples he went to Parma, where Azzo Correggio, with his wonted affection, pressed him to delay; and Petrarch accepted the invitation, though he remarked with sorrow that harmony no longer reigned among the brothers of the family. He stopped there, however, for some time, and enjoyed such tranquillity that he could revise and polish his compositions. But, in the following year, 1345, his friend Azzo, having failed to keep his promise to Luchino Visconti, as to restoring to him the lordship of Parma—Azzo had obtained it by the assistance of the Visconti, who avenged himself by making war on the Correggios—he invested Parma, and afflicted it with a tedious siege. Petrarch, foreseeing little prospect of pursuing his studies quietly in a beleaguered city, left the place with a small number of his companions; but, about midnight, near Rheggio, a troop of robbers rushed from an ambuscade, with cries of "Kill! kill!" and our handful of travellers, being no match for a host of brigands, fled and sought to save themselves under favour of night. Petrarch, during this flight, was thrown from his horse. The shock was so violent that he swooned; but he recovered, and was remounted by his companions. They had not got far, however, when a violent storm of rain and lightning rendered their situation almost as bad as that from which they had escaped, and threatened them with death in another shape. They passed a dreadful night without finding a tree or the hollow of a rock to shelter them, and had no expedient for mitigating their exposure to the storm but to turn their horses' backs to the tempest.

When the dawn permitted them to discern a path amidst the brushwood, they pushed on to Scandiano, a castle occupied by the Gonzaghi, friends of the lords of Parma, which they happily reached, and where they were kindly received. Here they learned that a troop of horse and foot had been waiting for them in ambush near Scandiano, but had been forced by the bad weather to withdraw before their arrival;

thus *"the pelting of the pitiless storm"* had been to them a merciful occurrence. Petrarch made no delay here, for he was smarting under the bruises from his fall, but caused himself to be tied upon his horse, and went to repose at Modena. The next day he repaired to Bologna, where he stopped a short time for surgical assistance, and whence he sent a letter to his friend Barbato, describing his misadventure; but, unable to hold a pen himself, he was obliged to employ the hand of a stranger. He was so impatient, however, to get back to Avignon, that he took the road to it as soon as he could sit his horse. On approaching that city he says he felt a greater softness in the air, and saw with delight the flowers that adorn the neighbouring woods. Everything seemed to announce the vicinity of Laura. It was seldom that Petrarch spoke so complacently of Avignon.

Clement VI. received Petrarch with the highest respect, offered him his choice among several vacant bishoprics, and pressed him to receive the office of pontifical secretary. He declined the proffered secretaryship. Prizing his independence above all things, excepting Laura, he remarked to his friends that the yoke of office would not sit lighter on him for being gilded.

In consequence of the dangers he had encountered, a rumour of his death had spread over a great part of Italy. The age was romantic, with a good deal of the fantastical in its romance. If the news had been true, and if he had been really dead and buried, it would be difficult to restrain a smile at the sort of honours that were paid to his memory by the less brain-gifted portion of his admirers. One of these, Antonio di Beccaria, a physician of Ferrara, when he ought to have been mourning for his own deceased patients, wrote a poetical lamentation for Petrarch's death. The poem, if it deserve such a name, is allegorical; it represents a funeral, in which the following personages parade in procession and grief for the Laureate's death. Grammar, Rhetoric, and Philosophy are introduced with their several attendants. Under the banners of Rhetoric are ranged Cicero, Geoffroy de Vinesauf, and Alain de Lisle. It would require all Cicero's eloquence to persuade us that his comrades in the procession were quite worthy of his company. The Nine Muses follow Petrarch's body; eleven poets, crowned with laurel, support the bier, and Minerva, holding the crown of Petrarch, closes the procession.

We have seen that Petrarch left Naples foreboding disastrous events to that kingdom. Among these, the assassination of Andrew, on the 18th of September, 1345, was one that fulfilled his augury. The particulars of this murder reached Petrarch on his arrival at Avignon, in a letter from his friend Barbato.

From the sonnets which Petrarch wrote, to all appearance, in 1345 and 1346, at Avignon or Vaucluse, he seems to have suffered from those fluctuations of Laura's favour that naturally arose from his own imprudence. When she treated him with affability, he grew bolder in his assiduities, and she was again obliged to be more severe. See Sonnets cviii., cix., and cxiv.

During this sojourn, though he dates some of his pleasantest letters from Vaucluse, he was projecting to return to Italy, and to establish himself there, after bidding a final adieu to Provence. When he acquainted his nominal patron, John Colonna, with his intention, the Cardinal rudely taxed him with madness and ingratitude. Petrarch frankly told the prelate that he was conscious of no ingratitude, since, after fourteen years passed in his service, he had received no provision for his future livelihood. This quarrel with the proud churchman is, with fantastic pastoral imagery, made the subject of our poet's eighth Bucolic, entitled Divortium. I suspect that Petrarch's free language in favour of the Tribune Rienzo was not unconnected with their alienation.

Notwithstanding Petrarch's declared dislike of Avignon, there is every reason to suppose that he passed the greater part of the winter of 1346 in his western Babylon; and we find that he witnessed many interesting scenes between the conflicting cardinals, as well as the brilliant fêtes that were given to two foreign princes, whom an important affair now brought to Avignon. These were the King of Bohemia, and his son Charles, Prince of Moravia, otherwise called Charles of Luxemburg.

The Emperor Lewis of Bavaria, who had previously made several but fruitless attempts to reconcile himself with the Church, on learning the election of Clement VI., sent ambassadors with unlimited powers to effect a reconcilement; but the Pope proposed conditions so hard and humbling that the States of the German Empire peremptorily rejected them. On this, his Holiness confirmed the condemnations which he had already passed on Lewis of Bavaria, and enjoined the Electors of the empire to proceed to a new choice of the King of the Romans. "John of Luxemburg," says Villani, "would have been emperor if he had not been blind." A wish to secure the empire for his son and to further his election, brought him to the Pope at Avignon.

Prince Charles had to thank the Pontiff for being elected, but first his Holiness made him sign, on the 22nd of April, 1346, in presence of twelve cardinals and his brother William Roger, a declaration of which the following is the substance:—

"If, by the grace of God, I am elected King of the Romans, I will fulfil all the promises and confirm all the concessions of my grandfather Henry VII. and of his predecessors. I will revoke the acts made by Lewis of Bavaria. I will occupy no place, either in or out of Italy, belonging to the Church. I will not enter Rome before the day appointed for my coronation. I will depart from thence the same day with all my attendants, and I will never return without the permission of the Holy See." He might as well have declared that he would give the Pope all his power, as King of the

Romans, provided he was allowed the profits; for, in reality, Charles had no other view with regard to Italy than to make money.

This concession, which contrasts so poorly with the conduct of Charles on many other occasions, excited universal indignation in Germany, and a good deal even in Italy. Petrarch exclaimed against it as mean and atrocious; for, Catholic as he was, he was not so much a churchman as to see without indignation the papal tiara exalted above the imperial crown.

In July, 1346, Charles was elected, and, in derision, was called "the Emperor of the Priests." The death of his rival, Lewis of Bavaria, however, which happened in the next year, prevented a civil war, and Charles IV. remained peaceable possessor of the empire.

Among the fêtes that were given to Charles, a ball was held at Avignon, in a grand saloon brightly illuminated. Thither came all the beauties of the city and of Provence. The Prince, who had heard much of Laura, through her poetical fame, sought her out and saluted her in the French manner.

Petrarch went, according to his custom, to pass the term of Lent at Vaucluse. The Bishop of Cavaillon, eager to see the poet, persuaded him to visit his recluse residence, and remained with Petrarch as his guest for fifteen days, in his own castle, on the summit of rocks, that seemed more adapted for the perch of birds than the habitation of men. There is now scarcely a wreck of it remaining.

It would seem, however, that the Bishop's conversation made this retirement very agreeable to Petrarch; for it inspired him with the idea of writing a "Treatise on a Solitary Life." Of this work he made a sketch in a short time, but did not finish it till twenty years afterwards, when he dedicated and presented it to the Bishop of Cavaillon.

It is agreeable to meet, in Petrarch's life at the shut-up valley, with any circumstance, however trifling, that indicates a cheerful state of mind; for, independently of his loneliness, the inextinguishable passion for Laura never ceased to haunt him; and his love, strange to say, had mad, momentary hopes, which only deepened at their departure the returning gloom of despair. Petrarch never wrote more sonnets on his beloved than during the course of this year. Laura had a fair and discreet female friend at Avignon, who was also the friend of Petrarch, and interested in his attachment. The ideas which this amiable confidante entertained of harmonizing success in misplaced attachment with honour and virtue must have been Platonic, even beyond the feelings which Petrarch, in reality, cherished; for, occasionally, the poet's sonnets are too honest for pure Platonism. This lady, however, whose name is unknown, strove to convince Laura that she ought to treat her lover with less severity. "She pushed Laura forward," says De Sade, "and kept back Petrarch." One day she recounted to the poet all the proofs of affection, and after these proofs she said, "You infidel, can you doubt that she loves you?" It is to this fair friend that he is supposed to have addressed his nineteenth sonnet.

This year, his Laura was seized with a defluxion in her eyes, which made her suffer much, and even threatened her with blindness. This was enough to bring a sonnet from Petrarch (his 94th), in which he laments that those eyes which were the sun of his life should be for ever eclipsed. He went to see her during her illness, having now the privilege of visiting her at her own house, and one day he found her perfectly recovered. Whether the ophthalmia was infectious, or only endemic, I know not; but so it was, that, whilst Laura's eyes got well, those of her lover became affected with the same defluxion. It struck his imagination, or, at least, he feigned to believe poetically, that the malady of her eyes had passed into his; and, in one of his sonnets, he exults at this welcome circumstance.[10] "I fixed my eyes," he said, "on Laura; and that moment a something inexpressible, like a shooting star, darted from them to mine. This is a present from love, in which I rejoice. How delightful it is thus to cure the darling object of one's soul!"

Petrarch received some show of complacency from Laura, which his imagination magnified; and it was some sort of consolation, at least, that his idol was courteous to him; but even this scanty solace was interrupted. Some malicious person communicated to Laura that Petrarch was imposing upon her, and that he was secretly addressing his love and his poetry to another lady under a borrowed name. Laura gave ear to the calumny, and, for a time, debarred him from her presence. If she had been wholly indifferent to him, this misunderstanding would have never existed; for jealousy and indifference are a contradiction in terms. I mean true jealousy. There is a pseudo species of it, with which many wives are troubled who care nothing about their husbands' affection; a plant of ill nature that is reared merely to be a rod of conjugal castigation. Laura, however, discovered at last, that her admirer was playing no double part. She was too reasonable to protract so unjust a quarrel, and received him again as usual.

I have already mentioned that Clement VI. had made Petrarch Canon of Modena, which benefice he resigned in favour of his friend, Luca Christino, and that this year his Holiness had also conferred upon him the prebend of Parma. This preferment excited the envy of some persons, who endeavoured to prejudice Ugolino de' Rossi, the bishop of the diocese, against him. Ugolino was of that family which had disputed for the sovereignty of Parma with the Correggios, and against whom Petrarch had pleaded in favour of their rivals. From this circumstance it was feared that Ugolino might be inclined to listen to those maligners who accused Petrarch of having gone to Avignon for the purpose of undermining the Bishop in the Pope's favour. Petrarch, upon his promotion, wrote a letter to Ugolino, strongly repelling this accusation. This is one of the manliest epistles that ever issued from his pen. "Allow me to assure you," he says, "that I would not exchange my tranquillity for your troubles, nor my poverty for your riches. Do not imagine, however, that I despise your particular situation. I only mean that there is no person of your rank whose preferment I desire; nor would I accept such preferment if it were offered to me. I should not say thus much, if my familiar intercourse with the Pope and the Cardinals had not convinced me that happiness in that rank is more a shadow than a substance. It was a memorable saying of Pope Adrian IV., 'that he knew no one more unhappy than the Sovereign Pontiff; his throne is a seat of thorns; his mantle is an oppressive weight; his tiara shines splendidly indeed, but it is not without a devouring fire.' If I had been ambitious," continues Petrarch, "I might have been preferred to a benefice of more value than yours;" and he refers to the fact of the Pope having given him his choice of several high preferments.

Petrarch passed the winter of 1346-47 chiefly at Avignon, and made but few and short excursions to Vaucluse. In one of these, at the beginning of 1347, when he had Socrates to keep him company at Vaucluse, the Bishop of Cavaillon invited them to his castle. Petrarch returned the following answer:—

"Yesterday we quitted the city of storms to take refuge in this harbour, and taste the sweets of repose. We have nothing but coarse clothes, suitable to the season and the place we live in; but in this rustic dress we will repair to see you, since you command us; we fear not to present ourselves in this rustic dress; our desire to see you puts down every other consideration. What matters it to us how we appear before one who possesses the depth of our hearts? If you wish to see us often you will treat us without ceremony."

His visits to Vaucluse were rather infrequent; business, he says, detained him often at Avignon, in spite of himself; but still at intervals he passed a day or two to look after his gardens and trees. On one of these occasions, he wrote a pleasing letter to William of Pastrengo, dilating on the pleasures of his garden, which displays liveliness and warmth of heart.

Petrarch had not seen his brother since the latter had taken the cowl in the Carthusian monastery, some five years before. To that convent he paid a visit in February, 1347, and he was received like an angel from heaven. He was delighted to see a brother whom he loved so much, and to find him contented with the life which he had embraced. The Carthusians, who had heard of Petrarch, renowned as the finest spirit of the age, were flattered by his showing a strong interest in their condition; and though he passed but a day and a night with them, they parted so mutually well pleased, that he promised, on taking leave, to send them a treatise on the happiness of the life which they led. And he kept his word; for, immediately upon his return to Vaucluse, he commenced his essay "*De Otio Religioso*—On the Leisure of the Religious," and he finished it in a few weeks. The object of this work is to show the sweets and advantages of their retired state, compared with the agitations of life in the world.

From these monkish reveries Petrarch was awakened by an astounding public event, namely, the elevation of Cola di Rienzo to the tribuneship of Rome. At the news of this revolution, Petrarch was animated with as much enthusiasm as if he had been himself engaged in the enterprise. Under the first impulse of his feelings, he sent an epistolary congratulation and advice to Rienzo and the Roman people. This letter breathes a strongly republican spirit. In later times, we perceive that Petrarch would have been glad to witness the accomplishment of his darling object—Rome restored to her ancient power and magnificence, even under an imperial government. Our poet received from the Tribune an answer to his epistolary oration, telling him that it had been read to the Roman people, and received with applause. A considerable number of letters passed between Petrarch and Cola.

When we look back on the long connection of Petrarch with the Colonna family, his acknowledged obligations, and the attachment to them which he expresses, it may seem, at first sight, surprising that he should have so loudly applauded a revolution which struck at the roots of their power. But, if we view the matter with a more considerate eye, we shall hold the poet in nobler and dearer estimation for his public zeal than if he had cringed to the Colonnas. His personal attachment to *them*, who were quite as much honoured by *his* friendship as *he* was by *theirs*, was a consideration subservient to that of the honour of his country and the freedom of his fellow-citizens; "for," as he says in his own defence, "we owe much to our friends, still more to our parents, but everything to our country."

Retiring during this year for some time to Vaucluse, Petrarch composed an eclogue in honour of the Roman revolution, the fifth in his Bucolics. It is entitled "La Pieta Pastorale," and has three speakers, who converse about their venerable mother Rome, but in so dull a manner, that, if Petrarch had never written better poetry, we should not, probably, at this moment, have heard of his existence.

In the midst of all this political fervour, the poet's devotion to Laura continued unabated; Petrarch never composed so many sonnets in one year as during 1347, but, for the most part, still indicative of sadness and despair. In his 116th sonnet, he says:
—

> "Soleo onde, e 'n rena fondo, e serivo in vento."
> I plough in water, build on sand, and write on air.

If anything were wanting to convince us that Laura had treated him, during his twenty years' courtship, with sufficient rigour, this and other such expressions would suffice to prove it. A lover, at the end of so long a period, is not apt to speak thus despondingly of a mistress who has been kind to him.

It seems, however, that there were exceptions to her extreme reserve. On one occasion, this year, when they met, and when Petrarch's eyes were fixed on her in silent reverie, she stretched out her hand to him, and allowed him to detain it in his for some time. This incident is alluded to in his 218th sonnet.

If public events, however, were not enough to make him forget his passion for Laura, they were sufficiently stirring to keep his interest in them alive. The head of Rienzo was not strong enough to stand the elevation which he had attained. Petrarch had hitherto regarded the reports of Rienzo's errors as highly exaggerated by his enemies; but the truth of them, at last, became too palpable; though our poet's charitable opinion of the Tribune considerably outlasted that of the public at large.

When the papal court heard of the multiplied extravagances of Rienzo, they recovered a little from the panic which had seized them. They saw that they had to deal with a man whose head was turned. His summonses had enraged them; and they resolved to keep no measures with him. Towards the end of August, 1347, one of his couriers arrived without arms, and with only the symbol of his office, the silver rod, in his hand. He was arrested near Avignon; his letters were taken from him and torn to pieces; and, without being permitted to enter Avignon, he was sent back to Rome with threats and ignominy. This proceeding appeared atrocious in the eyes of Petrarch, and he wrote a letter to Rienzo on the subject, expressing his strongest indignation at the act of outrage.

Coast of Genoa.

Petrarch passed almost the whole of the month of September, 1347, at Avignon. On the 9th of this month he obtained letters of legitimation for his son John, who might now be about ten years old. John is entitled, in these letters, "a scholar of Florence." The Pope empowers him to possess any kind of benefice without being obliged, in future, to make mention of his illegitimate birth, or of the obtained dispensation. It appears from these letters that the mother of John was not married. He left his son at Verona under the tuition of Rinaldo di Villa Franca. Before he had left Provence in this year, for the purpose of visiting Italy, he had announced his intention to the Pope, who wished to retain him as an honour to his court, and offered him his choice of several church preferments. But our poet, whose only wish was to obtain some moderate benefice that would leave him independent and at liberty, declined his Holiness's *vague* offers. If we consider that Petrarch made no secret of his good wishes for Rienzo, it may seem surprisingly creditable to the Pontiff's liberality that he should have even *professed* any interest in the poet's fortune; but in a letter to his friend Socrates, Petrarch gives us to understand that he thought the Pope's professions were merely verbal. He says: "To hold out treasures to a man who demands a small sum is but a polite mode of refusal." In fact, the Pope offered him *some* bishopric, knowing that he wanted only *some* benefice that should be a sinecure.

If it be asked what determined him now to leave Avignon, the counter-question may be put, what detained him so long from Italy? It appears that he had never parted with his house and garden at Parma; he hated everything in Avignon excepting Laura; and of the solitude of Vaucluse he was, in all probability, already weary.

Before he left Avignon, he went to take leave of Laura. He found her at an assembly which she often frequented. "She was seated," he says, "among those ladies who are generally her companions, and appeared like a beautiful rose surrounded with flowers smaller and less blooming." Her air was more touching than usual. She was dressed perfectly plain, and without pearls or garlands, or any gay colour. Though she was not melancholy, she did not appear to have her wonted cheerfulness, but was serious and thoughtful. She did not sing, as usual, nor speak with that voice which used to charm every one. She had the air of a person who fears an evil not yet arrived. "In taking leave of her," says Petrarch, "I sought in her looks for a consolation of my own sufferings. Her eyes had an expression which I had never seen in them before. What I saw in her face seemed to predict the sorrows that threatened me."

This was the last meeting that Petrarch and Laura ever had.

Petrarch set out for Italy, towards the close of 1347, having determined to make that country his residence for the rest of his life.

Upon his arrival at Genoa he wrote to Rienzo, reproaching him for his follies, and exhorting him to return to his former manly conduct. This advice, it is scarcely necessary to say, was like dew and sunshine bestowed upon barren sands.

From Genoa he proceeded to Parma, where he received the first information of the catastrophe of the Colonna family, six of whom had fallen in battle with Rienzo's forces. He showed himself deeply affected by it, and, probably, was so sincerely. But the Colonnas, though his former patrons, were still the enemies of a cause which he considered sacred, much as it was mismanaged and disgraced by the Tribune; and his grief cannot be supposed to have been immoderate. Accordingly, the letter which he wrote to Cardinal Colonna on this occasion is quite in the style of Seneca, and more like an ethical treatise than an epistle of condolence.

It is obvious that Petrarch slowly and reluctantly parted with his good opinion of Rienzo. But, whatever sentiments he might have cherished respecting him, he was now doomed to hear of his tragic fall.

The revolution which overthrew the Tribune was accomplished on the 15th of December, 1347. That his fall was, in a considerable degree, owing to his faults, is undeniable; and to the most contemptible of all faults—personal vanity. How hard it is on the great mass of mankind, that this meanness is so seldom disjoined from the zeal of popular championship! New power, like new wine, seems to intoxicate the strongest heads. How disgusting it is to see the restorer of Roman liberty dazzled like a child by a scarlet robe and its golden trimming! Nevertheless, with all his vanity, Rienzo was a better friend to the republic than those who dethroned him. The Romans would have been wise to have supported Rienzo, taking even his foibles into the account. They re-admitted their oligarchs; and, if they repented of it, as they did, they are scarcely entitled to our commiseration.

Petrarch had set out late in 1347 to visit Italy for the fifth time. He arrived at Genoa towards the end of November, 1347, on his way to Florence, where he was eagerly expected by his friends. They had obtained from the Government permission for his return; and he was absolved from the sentence of banishment in which he had been included with his father. But, whether Petrarch was offended with the Florentines for refusing to restore his paternal estate, or whether he was detained by accident in Lombardy, he put off his expedition to Florence and repaired to Parma. It was there that he learned the certainty of the Tribune's fall.

From Parma he went to Verona, where he arrived on the evening of the 25th of January, 1348. His son, we have already mentioned, was placed at Verona, under the tuition of Rinaldo di Villa Franca. Here, soon after his arrival, as he was sitting among his books, Petrarch felt the shock of a tremendous earthquake. It seemed as if the whole city was to be overturned from its foundations. He rushed immediately into the streets, where the inhabitants were gathered together in consternation; and, whilst terror was depicted in every countenance, there was a general cry that the end of the world was come. All contemporary historians mention this earthquake, and agree that it originated at the foot of the Alps. It made sad ravages at Pisa, Bologna, Padua, and Venice, and still more in the Frioul and Bavaria. If we may trust the narrators of this event, sixty villages in one canton were buried under two mountains that fell and filled up a valley five leagues in length. A whole castle, it is added, was exploded out of the earth from its foundation, and its ruins scattered many miles from the spot. The latter anecdote has undoubtedly an air of the marvellous; and yet the convulsions of nature have produced equally strange effects. Stones have been thrown out of Mount Ætna to the distance of eighteen miles.

The earthquake was the forerunner of awful calamities; and it is possible that it might be physically connected with that memorable plague in 1348, which reached, in succession, all parts of the known world, and thinned the population of every country which it visited. Historians generally agree that this great plague began in China and Tartary, whence, in the space of a year, it spread its desolation over the whole of Asia. It extended itself over Italy early in 1348; but its severest ravages had not yet been made, when Petrarch returned from Verona to Parma in the month of March, 1348. He brought with him his son John, whom he had withdrawn from the school of Rinaldo di Villa Franca, and placed under Gilberto di Parma, a good grammarian. His motive for this change of tutorship probably was, that he reckoned on Parma being henceforward his own principal place of residence, and his wish to have his son beside him.

Petrarch had scarcely arrived at Parma when he received a letter from Luchino Visconti, who had lately received the lordship of that city. Hearing of Petrarch's arrival there, the Prince, being at Milan, wrote to the poet, requesting some orange plants from his garden, together with a copy of verses. Petrarch sent him both, accompanied with a letter, in which he praises Luchino for his encouragement of learning and his cultivation of the Muses.

The plague was now increasing in Italy; and, after it had deprived Petrarch of many dear friends, it struck at the root of all his affections by attacking Laura. He describes his apprehensions on this occasion in several of his sonnets. The event confirmed his melancholy presages; for a letter from his friend Socrates informed him that Laura had died of the plague on the 1st of April, 1348. His biographers may well be believed, when they tell us that his grief was extreme. Laura's husband took the event more quietly, and consoled himself by marrying again, when only seven months a widower.

Petrarch, when informed of her death, wrote that marginal note upon his copy of Virgil, the authenticity of which has been so often, though unjustly, called in question. His words were the following:—

"Laura, illustrious for her virtues, and for a long time celebrated in my verses, for the first time appeared to my eyes on the 6th of April, 1327, in the church of St. Clara, at the first hour of the day. I was then in my youth. In the same city, and at the same hour, in the year 1348, this luminary disappeared from our world. I was then at Verona, ignorant of my wretched situation. Her chaste and beautiful body was buried the same day, after vespers, in the church of the Cordeliers. Her soul returned to its native mansion in heaven. I have written this with a pleasure mixed with bitterness, to retrace the melancholy remembrance of 'my great loss.' This loss convinces me that I have nothing now left worth living for, since the strongest cord of my life is broken. By the grace of God, I shall easily renounce a world where my hopes have been vain and perishing. It is time for me to fly from Babylon when the knot that bound me to it is untied."

This copy of Virgil is famous, also, for a miniature picture expressing the subject of the Æneid; which, by the common consent of connoisseurs in painting, is the work of Simone Memmi. Mention has already been made of the friendly terms that subsisted between that painter and our poet; whence it may be concluded that Petrarch, who received this precious MS. in 1338, requested of Simone this mark of his friendship, to render it more valuable.

When the library of Pavia, together with the city, was plundered by the French in 1499, and when many MSS. were carried away to the library of Paris, a certain inhabitant of Pavia had the address to snatch this copy of Virgil from the general rapine. This individual was, probably, Antonio di Pirro, in whose hands or house the Virgil continued till the beginning of the sixteenth century, as Vellutello attests in his article on the origin of Laura. From him it passed to Antonio Agostino; afterwards to Fulvio Orsino, who prized it very dearly. At Orsino's death it was bought at a high price by Cardinal Federigo Borromeo, and placed in the Ambrosian library, which had been founded by him with much care and at vast expense.

Until the year 1795, this copy of Virgil was celebrated only on account of the memorandum already quoted, and a few short marginal notes, written for illustrations of the text; but, a part of the same leaf having been torn and detached from the cover, the librarians, by chance, perceived some written characters. Curiosity urged them to unglue it with the greatest care; but the parchment was so conglutinated with the board that the letters left their impression on the latter so palely and weakly, that the librarians had great difficulty in making out the following notice, written by Petrarch himself: "Liber hic furto mihi subreptus fuerat, anno domini mcccxxvi., in Kalend. Novembr., ac deinde restitutus, anno mcccxxxvii., die xvii. Aprilis, apud Aivin⁰."

Then follows a note by the poet himself, regarding his son: "Johannes noster, natus ad laborem et dolorem meum, et vivens gravibus atque perpetuis me curis exercuit, et acri dolore moriens vulneravit, qui cum paucos et lætos dies vidisset in vita sua, decessit in anno domini 1361, ætatis suæ xxv., die Julii x. seu ix. medio noctis inter diem veneris et sabbati. Rumor ad me pervenerat xiii⁰ mensis ad vesperam, obiit autem Mlni illo publico excidio pestis insolito, quæ urbem illam, hactenus immunem, talibus malis nunc reperit atque invasit. Rumor autem primus ambiguus 8$^{vo.}$ Augusti, eodem anno, per famulum meum Mlno redeuntem, mox certus, per famulum Dom^{ni} Theatini Roma venientem 18$^{me.}$ mensis ejusdem Mercurii, sero ad me pervenit de obitu Socratis mei amici, socii fratrisque optimi, qui obiisse dicitur Babilone seu Avenione, die mense Maii proximo. Amisi comitem ac solatium vitæ meæ. Recipe Xte Ihu, hos duos et reliquos quinque in eterna tabernacula tua."[11] He alludes to the death of other friends; but the entire note is too long to be quoted, and, in many places, is obscured by contractions which make its meaning doubtful.

The perfect accordance of these memoranda with the other writings of the poet, conjoined with historical facts, show them incontestably to have come from the hand of Petrarch.

The precious MS. of Virgil, containing the autograph of Petrarch, is no longer in

Italy. Like many other relics held sacred by the Italians, it was removed by the French during the last conquest of Italy.

Among the incidents of Petrarch's life, in 1348, we ought to notice his visits to Giacomo da Carrara, whose family had supplanted the Della Scalas at Padua, and to Manfredi Pio, the Padrone of Carpi, a beautiful little city, of the Modenese territory, situated on a fine plain, on the banks of the Secchio, about four miles from Correggio. Manfredi ruled it with reputation for twenty years. Petrarch was magnificently received by the Carraras; and, within two years afterwards, they bestowed upon him the canonicate of Padua, a promotion which was followed in the same year by his appointment to the archdeaconry of Parma, of which he had been hitherto only canon.

Not long after the death of Laura, on the 3rd of July of the same year, Petrarch lost Cardinal Colonna, who had been for so many years his friend and patron. By some historians it is said that this prelate died of the plague; but Petrarch thought that he sank under grief brought on by the disasters of his family. In the space of five years the Cardinal had lost his mother and six brothers.

Petrarch still maintained an interest in the Colonna family, though that interest was against his own political principles, during the good behaviour of the Tribune. After the folly and fall of Rienzo, it is probable that our poet's attachment to his old friends of the Roman aristocracy revived. At least, he thought it decent to write, on the death of Cardinal Colonna, a letter of condolence to his father, the aged Stefano, who was now verging towards his hundredth year. Soon after this letter reached him, old Stefano fell into the grave.

The death of Cardinal Colonna was extremely felt at Avignon, where it left a great void, his house having been the rendezvous of men of letters and genius. Those who composed his court could not endure Avignon after they had lost their Mæcenas. Three of them were the particular friends of Petrarch, namely, Socrates, Luca Christine and Mainardo Accursio. Socrates, though not an Italian, was extremely embarrassed by the death of the Cardinal. He felt it difficult to live separated from Petrarch, and yet he could not determine to quit France for Italy. He wrote incessantly the most pressing letters to induce our poet to return and settle in Provence. Luca and Mainardo resolved to go and seek out Petrarch in Italy, in order to settle with him the place on which they should fix for their common residence, and where they should spend the rest of their lives in his society. They set out from Avignon in the month of March, 1349, and arrived at Parma, but did not find the poet, as he was gone on an excursion to Padua and Verona. They passed a day in his house to rest themselves, and, when they went away, left a letter in his library, telling him they had crossed the Alps to come and see him, but that, having missed him, as soon as they had finished an excursion which they meant to make, they would return and settle with him the means of their living together. Petrarch, on his return to Parma, wrote several interesting letters to Mainardo. In one of them he says, "I was much grieved that I had lost the pleasure of your company, and that of our worthy friend, Luca Christino. However, I am not without the consoling hope that my absence may be the means of hastening your return. As to your apprehensions about my returning to Vaucluse, I cannot deny that, at the entreaties of Socrates, I should return, provided I could procure an establishment in Provence, which would afford me an honourable pretence for residing there, and, at the same time, enable me to receive my friends with hospitality; but at present circumstances are changed. The Cardinal Colonna is dead, and my friends are all dispersed, excepting Socrates, who continues inviolably attached to Avignon.

"As to Vaucluse, I well know the beauties of that charming valley, and ten years' residence is a proof of my affection for the place. I have shown my love of it by the house which I built there. There I began my Africa, there I wrote the greater part of my epistles in prose and verse, and there I nearly finished all my eclogues. I never had so much leisure, nor felt so much enthusiasm, in any other spot. At Vaucluse I conceived the first idea of giving an epitome of the Lives of Illustrious Men, and there I wrote my Treatise on a Solitary Life, as well as that on religious retirement. It was there, also, that I sought to moderate my passion for Laura, which, alas, solitude only cherished. In short, this lonely valley will for ever be pleasing to my recollections. There is, nevertheless, a sad change, produced by time. Both the Cardinal and everything that is dear to me have perished. The veil which covered my eyes is at length removed. I can now perceive the difference between Vaucluse and the rich mountains and vales and flourishing cities of Italy. And yet, forgive me, so strong are the prepossessions of youth, that I must confess I pine for Vaucluse, even whilst I acknowledge its inferiority to Italy."

Whilst Petrarch was thus flattering his imagination with hopes that were never to be realized, his two friends, who had proceeded to cross the Apennines, came to an untimely fate. On the 5th of June, 1349, a servant, whom Petrarch had sent to inquire about some alarming accounts of the travellers that had gone abroad, returned sooner than he was expected, and showed by his face that he brought no pleasant tidings. Petrarch was writing—the pen fell from his hand. "What news do you bring?" "Very bad news! Your two friends, in crossing the Apennines, were attacked by robbers." "O God! what has happened to them?" The messenger replied, "Mainardo, who was behind his companions, was surrounded and murdered. Luca, hearing of his fate, came back sword in hand. He fought alone against ten, and he wounded some of the assailants, but at last he received many wounds, of which he lies almost dead. The robbers fled with their booty. The peasants assembled, and pursued, and would have captured them, if some gentlemen, unworthy of being called so, had not stopped the pursuit, and received the villains into their castles. Luca was seen among the rocks, but no one knows what is become of him." Petrarch, in the deepest agitation, despatched fleet couriers to Placenza, to Florence, and to Rome, to obtain intelligence about Luca.

These ruffians, who came from Florence, were protected by the Ubaldini, one of the most powerful and ancient families in Tuscany. As the murder was perpetrated within the territory of Florence, Petrarch wrote indignantly to the magistrates and people of that State, intreating them to avenge an outrage on their fellow citizens. Luca, it appears, expired of his wounds.

Petrarch's letter had its full effect. The Florentine commonwealth despatched soldiers, both horse and foot, against the Ubaldini and their banditti, and decreed that every year an expedition should be sent out against them till they should be routed out of their Alpine caverns. The Florentine troops directed their march to Monte Gemmoli, an almost impregnable rock, which they blockaded and besieged. The banditti issued forth from their strongholds, and skirmished with overmuch confidence in their vantage ground. At this crisis, the Florentine cavalry, having ascended the hill, dismounted from their horses, pushed forward on the banditti before they could retreat into their fortress, and drove them, sword in hand, within its inmost circle. The Florentines thus possessed themselves of Monte Gemmoli, and, in like manner, of several other strongholds. There were others which they could not take by storm, but they laid waste the plains and cities which supplied the robbers with provisions; and, after having done great damage to the Ubaldini, they returned safe and sound to Florence.

While Petrarch was at Mantua, in February, 1350, the Cardinal Guy of Boulogne, legate of the holy see, arrived there after a papal mission to Hungary. Petrarch was much attached to him. The Cardinal and several eminent persons who attended him had frequent conversations with our poet, in which they described to him the state of Germany and the situation of the Emperor.

Clement VI., who had reason to be satisfied with the submissiveness of this Prince, wished to attract him into Italy, where he hoped to oppose him to the Visconti, who had put themselves at the head of the Ghibeline party, and gave much annoyance to the Guelphs. His Holiness strongly solicited him to come; but Charles's situation would not permit him for the present to undertake such an expedition. There were still some troubles in Germany that remained to be appeased; besides, the Prince's purse was exhausted by the largesses which he had paid for his election, and his poverty was extreme.

It must be owned that a prince in such circumstances could hardly be expected to set out for the subjugation of Italy. Petrarch, however, took a romantic view of the Emperor's duties, and thought that the restoration of the Roman empire was within Charles's grasp. Our poet never lost sight of his favourite chimera, the re-establishment of Rome in her ancient dominion. It was what he called one of his principles, that Rome had a right to govern the world. Wild as this vision was, he had seen Rienzo attempt its realization; and, if the Tribune had been more prudent, there is no saying how nearly he might have approached to the achievement of so marvellous an issue. But Rienzo was fallen irrecoverably, and Petrarch now desired as ardently to see the Emperor in Italy, as ever he had sighed for the success of the Tribune. He wrote to the Emperor a long letter from Padua, a few days after the departure of the Cardinal.

"I am agitated," he says, "in sending this epistle, when I think from whom it comes, and to whom it is addressed. Placed as I am, in obscurity, I am dazzled by the splendour of your name; but love has banished fear: this letter will at least make known to you my fidelity, and my zeal. Read it, I conjure you! You will not find in it the insipid adulation which is the plague of monarchs. Flattery is an art unknown to me. I have to offer you only complaints and regrets. You have forgotten us. I say more—you have forgotten yourself in neglecting Italy. We had high hopes that Heaven had sent you to restore us our liberty; but it seems that you refuse this mission, and, whilst the time should be spent in acting, you lose it in deliberating.

"You see, Cæsar, with what confidence an obscure man addresses you, a man who has not even the advantage of being known to you. But, far from being offended with the liberty I take, you ought rather to thank your own character, which inspires me with such confidence. To return to my subject—wherefore do you lose time in consultation? To all appearance, you are sure of the future, if you will avail yourself of the present. You cannot be ignorant that the success of great affairs often hangs upon an instant, and that a day has been frequently sufficient to consummate what it required ages to undo. Believe me, your glory and the safety of the commonwealth, your own interests, as well as ours, require that there be no delay. You are still young, but time is flying; and old age will come and take you by surprise when you are at least expecting it. Are you afraid of too soon commencing an enterprise for which a long life would scarcely suffice?

"The Roman empire, shaken by a thousand storms, and as often deceived by fallacious calms, places at last its whole hopes in you. It recovers a little breath even under the shelter of your name; but hope alone will not support it. In proportion as you know the grandeur of the undertaking, consummate it the sooner. Let not the love of your Transalpine dominions detain you longer. In beholding Germany, think of Italy. If the one has given you birth, the other has given you greatness. If you are king of the one, you are king and emperor of the other. Let me say, without meaning offence to other nations, that here is the head of your monarchy. Everywhere else you will find only its members. What a glorious project to unite those members to their head!

"I am aware that you dislike all innovation; but what I propose would be no innovation on your part. Italy is as well known to you as Germany. Brought hither in your youth by your illustrious sire, he made you acquainted with our cities and our manners, and taught you here the first lessons of war. In the bloom of your youth, you have obtained great victories. Can you fear at present to enter a country where you have triumphed since your childhood?

"By the singular favour of Heaven we have regained the ancient right of being governed by a prince of our own nation.[12] Let Germany say what she will, Italy is veritably your country * * * * * Come with haste to restore peace to Italy. Behold Rome, once the empress of the world, now pale, with scattered locks and torn garments, at your feet, imploring your presence and support!" Then follows a dissertation on the history and heroes of Rome, which might be wearisome if transcribed to a modern reader. But the epistle, upon the whole, is manly and eloquent.

A few days after despatching his letter to the Emperor, Petrarch made a journey to Verona to see his friends. There he wrote to Socrates. In this letter, after enumerating the few friends whom the plague had spared, he confesses that he could not flatter himself with the hope of being able to join them in Provence. He therefore invokes them to come to Italy, and to settle either at Parma or at Padua, or any other place that would suit them. His remaining friends, here enumerated, were only Barbato of Sulmona, Francesco Rinucci, John Boccaccio, Lælius, Guido Settimo, and Socrates.

Petrarch had returned to Padua, there to rejoin the Cardinal of Boulogne. The Cardinal came back thither at the end of April, 1350, and, after dispensing his blessings, spiritual and temporal, set out for Avignon, travelling by way of Milan and Genoa. Petrarch accompanied the prelate out of personal attachment on a part of his journey. The Cardinal was fond of his conversation, but sometimes rallied the poet on his enthusiasm for his native Italy. When they reached the territory of Verona, near the lake of Guarda, they were struck by the beauty of the prospect, and stopped to contemplate it. In the distance were the Alps, topped with snow even in summer. Beneath was the lake of Guarda, with its flux and reflux, like the sea, and around them were the rich hills and fertile valleys. "It must be confessed," said the Legate to Petrarch, "that your country is more beautiful than ours." The face of Petrarch brightened up. "But you must agree," continued the Cardinal, perhaps to moderate the poet's exultation, "that ours is more tranquil." "That is true," replied Petrarch, "but we can obtain tranquillity whenever we choose to come to our senses, and desire peace, whereas you cannot procure those beauties which nature has lavished *on us.*"

Petrarch here took leave of the Cardinal, and set out for Parma. Taking Mantua in his way, he set out from thence in the evening, in order to sleep at Luzora, five leagues from the Po. The lords of that city had sent a courier to Mantua, desiring that he would honour them with his presence at supper. The melting snows and the overflowing river had made the roads nearly impassable; but he reached the place in time to avail himself of the invitation. His hosts gave him a magnificent reception. The supper was exquisite, the dishes rare, the wines delicious, and the company full of gaiety. But a small matter, however, will spoil the finest feast. The supper was served up in a damp, low hall, and all sorts of insects annoyed the convivials. To crown their misfortune an army of frogs, attracted, no doubt, by the odour of the meats, crowded and croaked about them, till they were obliged to leave their unfinished supper.

Petrarch returned next day for Parma. We find, from the original fragments of his poems, brought to light by Ubaldini, that he was occupied in retouching them during the summer which he passed at Parma, waiting for the termination of the excessive heats, to go to Rome and attend the jubilee. With a view to make the journey pleasanter, he invited Guglielmo di Pastrengo to accompany him, in a letter written in Latin verse. Nothing would have delighted Guglielmo more than a journey to Rome with Petrarch; but he was settled at Verona, and could not absent himself from his family.

In lieu of Pastrengo, Petrarch found a respectable old abbot, and several others who were capable of being agreeable, and from their experience, useful companions to him on the road. In the middle of October, 1350, they departed from Florence for Rome, to attend the jubilee. On his way between Bolsena and Viterbo, he met with an accident which threatened dangerous consequences, and which he relates in a letter to Boccaccio.

"On the 15th of October," he says, "we left Bolsena, a little town scarcely known at present; but interesting from having been anciently one of the principal places in Etruria. Occupied with the hopes of seeing Rome in five days, I reflected on the changes in our modes of thinking which are made by the course of years. Fourteen years ago I repaired to the great city from sheer curiosity to see its wonders. The second time I came was to receive the laurel. My third and fourth journey had no object but to render services to my persecuted friends. My present visit ought to be more happy, since its only object is my eternal salvation." It appears, however, that the horses of the travellers had no such devotional feelings; "for," he continues, "whilst my mind was full of these thoughts, the horse of the old abbot, which was walking upon my left, kicking at my horse, struck me upon the leg, just below the knee. The blow was so violent that it sounded as if a bone was broken. My attendants came up. I felt an acute pain, which made me, at first, desirous of stopping; but, fearing the dangerousness of the place, I made a virtue of necessity, and went on to Viterbo, where we arrived very late on the 16th of October. Three days afterwards they dragged me to Rome with much trouble. As soon as I arrived at Rome, I called for doctors, who found the bone laid bare. It was not, however, thought to be broken; though the shoe of the horse had left its impression."

However impatient Petrarch might be to look once more on the beauties of Rome, and to join in the jubilee, he was obliged to keep his bed for many days.

The concourse of pilgrims to this jubilee was immense. One can scarcely credit the common account that there were about a million pilgrims at one time assembled in the great city. "We do not perceive," says Petrarch, "that the plague has depopulated the world." And, indeed, if this computation of the congregated pilgrims approaches the truth, we cannot but suspect that the alleged depopulation of Europe, already mentioned, must have been exaggerated. "The crowds," he continues, "diminished a little during summer and the gathering-in of the harvest; but recommenced towards the end of the year. The great nobles and ladies from beyond the Alps came the last."

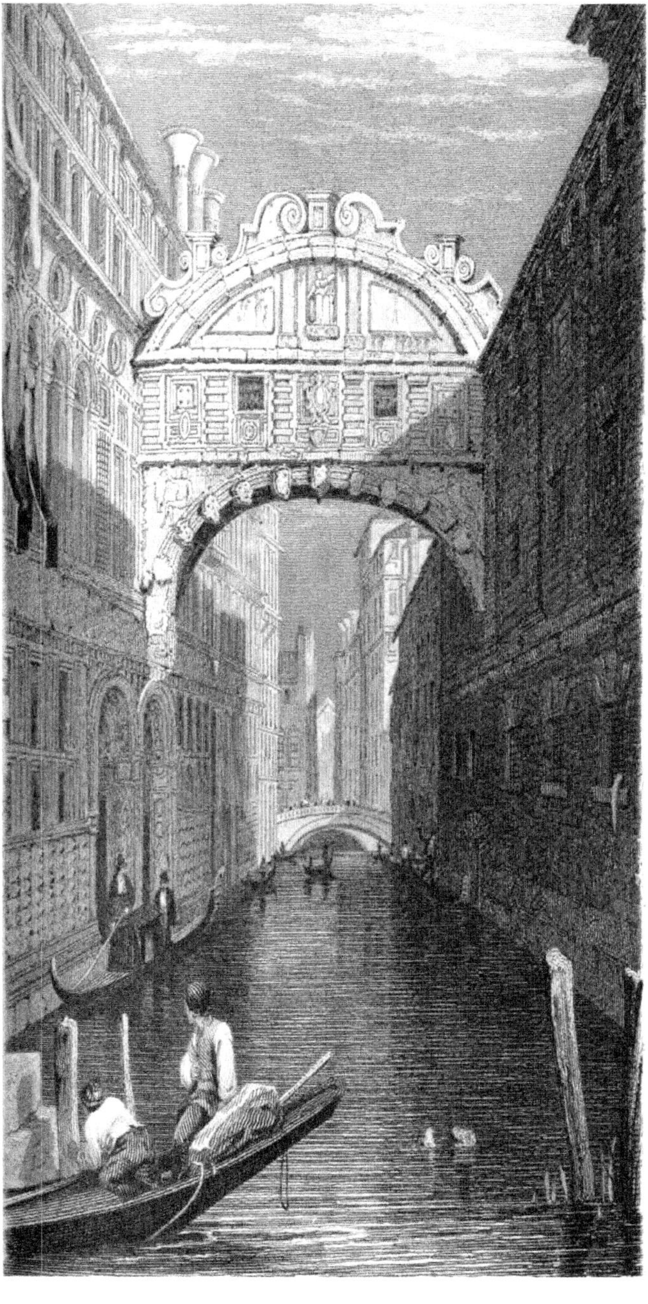

Bridge of Sighs,—Venice.

Many of the female pilgrims arrived by way of the marshes of Ancona, where Bernardino di Roberto, Lord of Ravenna, waited for them, and scandal whispered that his assiduities and those of his suite were but too successful in seducing them. A contemporary author, in allusion to the circumstance, remarks that journeys and indulgences are not good for young persons, and that the fair ones had better have remained at home, since the vessel that stays in port is never shipwrecked.

The strangers, who came from all countries, were for the most part unacquainted with the Italian language, and were obliged to employ interpreters in making their confession, for the sake of obtaining absolution. It was found that many of the pretended interpreters were either imperfectly acquainted with the language of the foreigners, or were knaves in collusion with the priestly confessors, who made the poor pilgrims confess whatever they chose, and pay for their sins accordingly. A better subject for a scene in comedy could scarcely be imagined. But, to remedy this abuse, penitentiaries were established at Rome, in which the confessors understood foreign languages.

The number of days fixed for the Roman pilgrims to visit the churches was thirty; and fifteen or ten for the Italians and other strangers, according to the distance of the places from which they came.

Petrarch says that it is inconceivable how the city of Rome, whose adjacent fields were untilled, and whose vineyards had been frozen the year before, could for twelve months support such a confluence of people. He extols the hospitality of the citizens, and the abundance of food which prevailed; but Villani and others give us more disagreeable accounts—namely, that the Roman citizens became hotel-keepers, and charged exorbitantly for lodgings, and for whatever they sold. Numbers of pilgrims were thus necessitated to live poorly; and this, added to their fatigue and the heats of summer, produced a great mortality.

As soon as Petrarch, relieved by surgical skill from the wound in his leg, was allowed to go out, he visited all the churches.

After having performed his duties at the jubilee, Petrarch returned to Padua, taking the road by Arezzo, the town which had the honour of his birth. Leonardo Aretino says that his fellow-townsmen crowded around him with delight, and received him with such honours as could have been paid only to a king.

In the same month of December, 1350, he discovered a treasure which made him happier than a king. Perhaps a royal head might not have equally valued it. It was a copy of Quintilian's work "De Institutione Oratoria," which, till then, had escaped all his researches. On the very day of the discovery he wrote a letter to Quintilian, according to his fantastic custom of epistolizing the ancients. Some days afterwards, he left Arezzo to pursue his journey. The principal persons of the town took leave of him publicly at his departure, after pointing out to him the house in which he was born. "It was a small house," says Petrarch, "befitting an exile, as my father was." They told him that the proprietors would have made some alterations in it; but the town had interposed and prevented them, determined that the place should remain the same as when it was first consecrated by his birth. The poet related what had been mentioned to a young man who wrote to him expressly to ask whether Arezzo could really boast of being his birthplace. Petrarch added, that Arezzo had done more for him as a stranger than Florence as a citizen. In truth, his family was of Florence; and it was only by accident that he was born at Arezzo. He then went to Florence, where he made but a short stay. There he found his friends still alarmed about the accident which had befallen him in his journey to Rome, the news of which he had communicated to Boccaccio.

Petrarch went on to Padua. On approaching it, he perceived a universal mourning. He soon learned the foul catastrophe which had deprived the city of one of its best masters.

Jacopo di Carrara had received into his house his cousin Guglielmo. Though the latter was known to be an evil-disposed person, he was treated with kindness by Jacopo, and ate at his table. On the 21st of December, whilst Jacopo was sitting at supper, in the midst of his friends, his people and his guards, the monster Guglielmo plunged a dagger into his breast with such celerity, that even those who were nearest could not ward off the blow. Horror-struck, they lifted him up, whilst others put the assassin to instant death.

The fate of Jacopo Carrara gave Petrarch a dislike for Padua, and his recollections of Vaucluse bent his unsettled mind to return to its solitude; but he tarried at Padua during the winter. Here he spent a great deal of his time with Ildebrando Conti, bishop of that city, a man of rank and merit. One day, as he was dining at the Bishop's palace, two Carthusian monks were announced: they were well received by the Bishop, as he was partial to their order. He asked them what brought them to Padua. "We are going," they said, "to Treviso, by the direction of our general, there to remain and establish a monastery." Ildebrando asked if they knew Father Gherardo, Petrarch's brother. The two monks, who did not know the poet, gave the most pleasing accounts of his brother.

The plague, they said, having got into the convent of Montrieux, the prior, a pious but timorous man, told his monks that flight was the only course which they could take: Gherardo answered with courage, "Go whither you please! As for myself I will remain in the situation in which Heaven has placed me." The prior fled to his own country, where death soon overtook him. Gherardo remained in the convent, where the plague spared him, and left him alone, after having destroyed, within a few days, thirty-four of the brethren who had continued with him. He paid them every service, received their last sighs, and buried them when death had taken off those to whom that office belonged. With only a dog left for his companion, Gherardo watched at night to guard the house, and took his repose by day. When the summer was over, he went to a neighbouring monastery of the Carthusians, who enabled him to restore his convent.

While the Carthusians were making this honourable mention of Father Gherardo, the prelate cast his eyes from time to time upon Petrarch. "I know not," says the poet, "whether my eyes were filled with tears, but my heart was tenderly touched." The Carthusians, at last discovering who Petrarch was, saluted him with congratulations. Petrarch gives an account of this interview in a letter to his brother himself.

Padua was too near to Venice for Petrarch not to visit now and then that city which he called the wonder of the world. He there made acquaintance with Andrea Dandolo, who was made Doge in 1343, though he was only thirty-six years of age, an extraordinary elevation for so young a man; but he possessed extraordinary merit. His mind was cultivated; he loved literature, and easily became, as far as mutual demonstrations went, the personal friend of Petrarch; though the Doge, as we shall see, excluded this personal friendship from all influence on his political conduct.

The commerce of the Venetians made great progress under the Dogeship of Andrea Dandolo. It was then that they began to trade with Egypt and Syria, whence they brought silk, pearls, the spices, and other products of the East. This prosperity excited the jealousy of the Genoese, as it interfered with a commerce which they had hitherto monopolized. When the Venetians had been chased from Constantinople by the Emperor Michael Paleologus, they retained several fortresses in the Black Sea, which enabled them to continue their trade with the Tartars in that sea, and to frequent the fair of Tana. The Genoese, who were masters of Pera, a suburb of Constantinople, would willingly have joined the Greeks in expelling their Italian rivals altogether from the Black Sea; and privateering hostilities actually commenced between the two republics, which, in 1350, extended to the serious aspect of a national war.

The winter of that year was passed on both sides in preparations. The Venetians sent ambassadors to the King of Arragon, who had some differences with the Genoese about the Island of Sardinia, and to the Emperor of Constantinople, who saw with any sensation in the world but delight the flag of Genoa flying over the walls of Pera. A league between those three powers was quickly concluded, and their grand, common object was to destroy the city of Genoa.

It was impossible that these great movements of Venice should be unknown at Padua. Petrarch, ever zealous for the common good of Italy, saw with pain the kindling of a war which could not but be fatal to her, and thought it his duty to open his heart to the Doge of Venice, who had shown him so much friendship. He addressed to him, therefore, the following letter from Padua, on the 14th of March, 1351:—

"My love for my country forces me to break silence; the goodness of your character encourages me. Can I hold my peace whilst I hear the symptoms of a coming storm that menaces my beloved country? Two puissant people are flying to arms; two flourishing cities are agitated by the approach of war. These cities are placed by nature like the two eyes of Italy; the one in the south and west, and the other in the east and north, to dominate over the two seas that surround them; so that, even after the destruction of the Roman empire, this beautiful country was still regarded as the queen of the world. I know that proud nations denied her the empire of the land, but who dared ever to dispute with her the empire of the sea?

"I shudder to think of our prospects. If Venice and Genoa turn their victorious arms against each other, it is all over with us; we lose our glory and the command of the sea. In this calamity we shall have a consolation which we have ever had, namely, that if our enemies rejoice in our calamities, they cannot at least derive any glory from them.

"In great affairs I have always dreaded the counsels of the young. Youthful ignorance and inexperience have been the ruin of many empires. I, therefore, learn with pleasure that you have named a council of elders, to whom you have confided this affair. I expected no less than this from your wisdom, which is far beyond your years.

"The state of your republic distresses me. I know the difference that there is between the tumult of arms and the tranquillity of Parnassus. I know that the sounds of Apollo's lyre accord but ill with the trumpets of Mars; but if you have abandoned Parnassus, it has been only to fulfil the duties of a good citizen and of a vigilant chief. I am persuaded, at the same time, that in the midst of arms you think of peace; that you would regard it as a triumph for yourself, and the greatest blessing you could procure for your country. Did not Hannibal himself say that a sure peace was more valuable than a hoped-for victory! If truth has extorted this confession from the most warlike man that ever lived, is it not plain that a pacific man ought to prefer peace even to a certain victory? Who does not know that peace is the greatest of blessings, and that war is the source of all evils?

"Do not deceive yourself; you have to deal with a keen people who know not what it is to be conquered. Would it not be better to transfer the war to Damascus, to Susa, or to Memphis? Think besides, that those whom you are going to attack are your brothers. At Thebes, of old, two brothers fought to their mutual destruction. Must Italy renew, in our days, so atrocious a spectacle?

"Let us examine what may be the results of this war. Whether you are conqueror or are conquered, one of the eyes of Italy will necessarily be blinded, and the other much weakened; for it would be folly to flatter yourself with the hopes of conquering so strong an enemy without much effusion of blood.

"Brave men, powerful people! (I speak here to both of you) what is your object— to what do you aspire? What will be the end of your dissensions? It is not the blood of the Carthaginians or the Numantians that you are about to spill, but it is Italian blood; the blood of a people who would be the first to start up and offer to expend their blood, if any barbarous nation were to attempt a new irruption among us. In that event, their bodies would be the bucklers and ramparts of our common country; they would live, or they would die with us. Ought the pleasure of avenging a slight offence to carry more weight with you than the public good and your own safety? Let revenge be the delight of women. Is it not more glorious for men to forget an injury than to avenge it? to pardon an enemy than to destroy him?

"If my feeble voice could make itself heard among those grave men who compose your council, I am persuaded that you would not only *not* reject the peace which is offered to you, but go to meet and embrace it closely, so that it might not escape you. Consult your wise old men who love the republic; they will speak the same language to you that I do.

"You, my lord, who are at the head of the council, and who govern your republic, ought to recollect that the glory or the shame of these events will fall principally on you. Raise yourself above yourself; look into, examine everything with attention. Compare the success of the war with the evils which it brings in its train. Weigh in a balance the good effects and the evil, and you will say with Hannibal, that an hour is sufficient to destroy the work of many years.

"The renown of your country is more ancient than is generally believed. Several ages before the city of Venice was built, I find not only the name of the Venetians famous, but also that of one of their dukes. Would you submit to the caprices of fortune a glory acquired for so long a time, and at so great a cost? You will render a great service to your republic, if, preferring her safety to her glory, you give her incensed and insane populace prudent and useful counsels, instead of offering them brilliant and specious projects. The wise say that we cannot purchase a virtue more precious than what is bought at the expense of glory. If you adopt this axiom, your character will be handed down to posterity, like that of the Duke of the Venetians, to whom I have alluded. All the world will admire and love you.

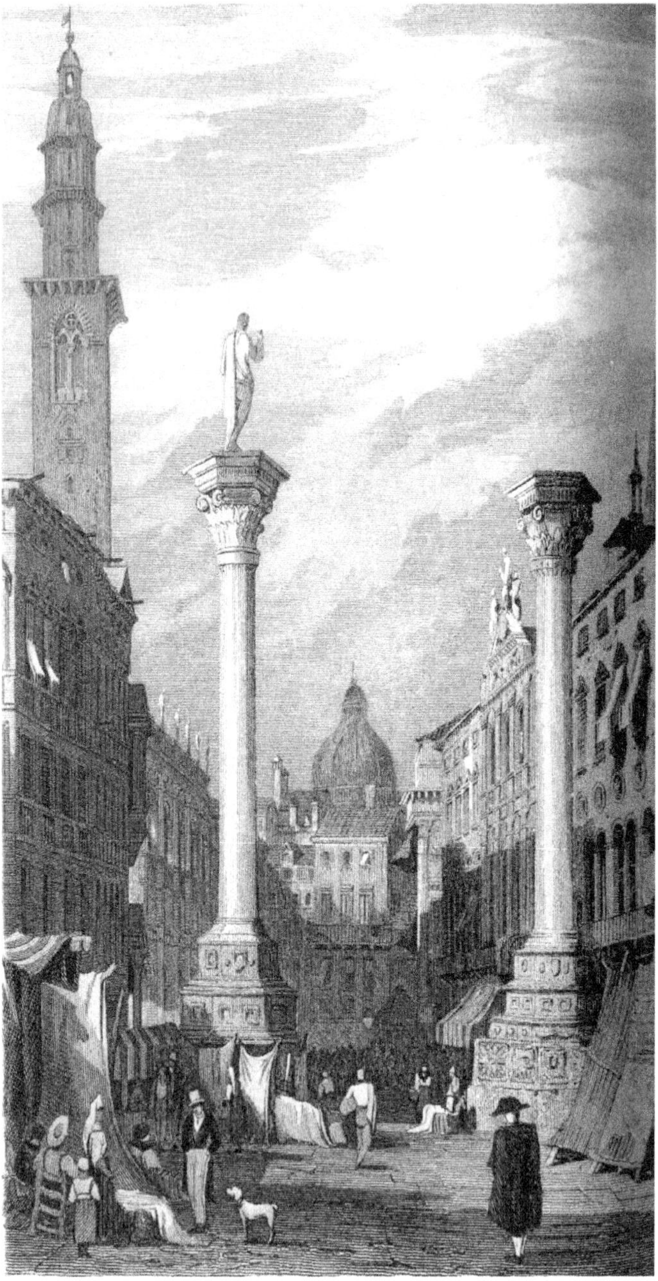

Vicenza.

"To conceal nothing from you, I confess that I have heard with grief of your league with the King of Arragon. What! shall Italians go and implore succour of barbarous kings to destroy Italians? You will say, perhaps, that your enemies have set you the example. My answer is, that they are equally culpable. According to report, Venice, in order to satiate her rage, calls to her aid tyrants of the west; whilst Genoa brings in those of the east. This is the source of our calamities. Carried away by the admiration of strange things, despising, I know not why, the good things which we find in our own climate, we sacrifice sound Italian faith to barbarian perfidy. Madmen that we are, we seek among venal souls that which we could find among our own brethren.

"Nature has given us for barriers the Alps and the two seas. Avarice, envy, and pride, have opened these natural defences to the Cimbri, the Huns, the Goths, the Gauls, and the Spaniards. How often have we recited the words of Virgil:—

> "'Impius hæc tam culta novalia miles habebit,
> Barbarus has segetes.'

"Athens and Lacedemon had between them a species of rivalship similar to yours: but their forces were not by any means so nearly balanced. Lacedemon had an advantage over Athens, which put it in the power of the former to destroy her rival, if she had wished it; but she replied, 'God forbid that I should pull out one of the eyes of Greece!' If this beautiful sentiment came from a people whom Plato reproaches with their avidity for conquest and dominion, what still softer reply ought we not to expect from the most modest of nations!

"Amidst the movements which agitate you, it is impossible for me to be tranquil. When I see one party cutting down trees to construct vessels, and others sharpening their swords and darts, I should think myself guilty if I did not seize my pen, which is my only weapon, to counsel peace. I am aware with what circumspection we ought to speak to our superiors; but the love of our country has no superior. If it should carry me beyond bounds, it will serve as my excuse before you, and oblige you to pardon me.

"Throwing myself at the feet of the chiefs of two nations who are going to war, I say to them, with tears in my eyes, 'Throw away your arms; give one another the embrace of peace! unite your hearts and your colours. By this means the ocean and the Euxine shall be open to you. Your ships will arrive in safety at Taprobane, at the Fortunate Isles, at Thule, and even at the poles. The kings and their people will meet you with respect; the Indian, the Englishman, the Æthiopian, will dread you. May peace reign among you, and may you have nothing to fear!' Adieu! greatest of dukes, and best of men!"

This letter produced no effect. Andrea Dandolo, in his answer to it, alleges the thousand and one affronts and outrages which Venice had suffered from Genoa. At the same time he pays a high compliment to the eloquence of Petrarch's epistle, and says that it is a production which could emanate only from a mind inspired by the divine Spirit.

During the spring of this year, 1351, Petrarch put his last finish to a canzone, on the subject still nearest to his heart, the death of his Laura, and to a sonnet on the same subject. In April, his attention was recalled from visionary things by the arrival of Boccaccio, who was sent by the republic of Florence to announce to him the recall of his family to their native land, and the restoration of his family fortune, as well as to invite him to the home of his ancestors, in the name of the Florentine republic. The invitation was conveyed in a long and flattering letter; but it appeared, from the very contents of this epistle, that the Florentines wished our poet's acceptance of their offer to be as advantageous to themselves as to him. They were establishing a University, and they wished to put Petrarch at the head of it. Petrarch replied in a letter apparently full of gratitude and satisfaction, but in which he by no means pledged himself to be the gymnasiarch of their new college; and, agreeably to his original intention, he set out from Padua on the 3rd of May, 1351, for Provence.

Petrarch took the road to Vicenza, where he arrived at sunset. He hesitated whether he should stop there, or take advantage of the remainder of the day and go farther. But, meeting with some interesting persons whose conversation beguiled him, night came on before he was aware how late it was. Their conversation, in the course of the evening, ran upon Cicero. Many were the eulogies passed on the great old Roman; but Petrarch, after having lauded his divine genius and eloquence, said something about his inconsistency. Every one was astonished at our poet's boldness, but particularly a man, venerable for his age and knowledge, who was an idolater of Cicero. Petrarch argued pretty freely against the political character of the ancient orator. The same opinion as to Cicero's weakness seems rather to have gained ground in later ages. At least, it is now agreed that Cicero's political life will not bear throughout an uncharitable investigation, though the political difficulties of his time demand abundant allowance.

Petrarch departed next morning for Verona, where he reckoned on remaining only for a few days; but it was impossible for him to resist the importunities of Azzo Correggio, Guglielmo di Pastrengo, and his other friends. By them he was detained during the remainder of the month. "The requests of a friend," he said, on this occasion, "are always chains upon me."

Petrarch arrived, for the sixth time, at Vaucluse on the 27th of June, 1351. He first announced himself to Philip of Cabassoles, Bishop of Cavaillon, to whom he had already sent, during his journey, some Latin verses, in which he speaks of Vaucluse as the most charming place in the universe. "When a child," he says, "I visited it, and it nourished my youth in its sunny bosom. When grown to manhood, I passed some of the pleasantest years of my life in the shut-up valley. Grown old, I wish to pass in it my last years."

The sight of his romantic hermitage, of the capacious grotto which had listened to his sighs for Laura, of his garden, and of his library, was, undoubtedly, sweet to Petrarch; and, though he had promised Boccaccio to come back to Italy, he had not the fortitude to determine on a sudden return. He writes to one of his Italian friends, "When I left my native country, I promised to return to it in the autumn; but time, place, and circumstances, often oblige us to change our resolutions. As far as I can judge, it will be necessary for me to remain here for two years. My friends in Italy, I trust, will pardon me if I do not keep my promise to them. The inconstancy of the human mind must serve as my excuse. I have now experienced that change of place is the only thing which can long keep from us the *ennui* that is inseparable from a sedentary life."

At the same time, whilst Vaucluse threw recollections tender, though melancholy, over Petrarch's mind, it does not appear that Avignon had assumed any new charm in his absence: on the contrary, he found it plunged more than ever in luxury, wantonness, and gluttony. Clement VI. had replenished the church, at the request of the French king, with numbers of cardinals, many of whom were so young and licentious, that the most scandalous abominations prevailed amongst them. "At this time," says Matthew Villani, "no regard was paid either to learning or virtue; and a man needed not to blush for anything, if he could cover his head with a red hat. Pietro Ruggiero, one of those exemplary new cardinals, was only eighteen years of age." Petrarch vented his indignation on this occasion in his seventh eclogue, which is a satire upon the Pontiff and his cardinals, the interlocutors being Micione, or Clement himself, and Epi, or the city of Avignon. The poem, if it can be so called, is clouded with allegory, and denaturalized with pastoral conceits; yet it is worth being explored by any one anxious to trace the first fountains of reform among Catholics, as a proof of church abuses having been exposed, two centuries before the Reformation, by a Catholic and a churchman.

At this crisis, the Court of Avignon, which, in fact, had not known very well what to do about the affairs of Rome, were now anxious to inquire what sort of government would be the most advisable, after the fall of Rienzo. Since that event, the Cardinal Legate had re-established the ancient government, having created two senators, the one from the house of Colonna, the other from that of the Orsini. But, very soon, those houses were divided by discord, and the city was plunged into all the evils which it had suffered before the existence of the Tribuneship. "The community at large," says Matthew Villani, "returned to such condition, that strangers and travellers found themselves like sheep among wolves." Clement VI. was weary of seeing the metropolis of Christianity a prey to anarchy. He therefore chose four cardinals, whose united deliberations might appease these troubles, and he imagined that he could establish in Rome a form of government that should be durable. The cardinals requested Petrarch to give his opinion on this important affair. Petrarch wrote to them a most eloquent epistle, full of enthusiastic ideas of the grandeur of Rome. It is not exactly known what effect he produced by his writing on this subject; but on that account we are not to conclude that he wrote in vain.

Petrarch had brought to Avignon his son John, who was still very young. He had obtained for him a canonicate at Verona. Thither he immediately despatched him, with letters to Guglielmo di Pastrengo and Rinaldo di Villa Franca, charging the former of these friends to superintend his son's general character and manners, and the other to cultivate his understanding. Petrarch, in his letter to Rinaldo, gives a description of John, which is neither very flattering to the youth, nor calculated to give us a favourable opinion of his father's mode of managing his education. By his own account, it appears that he had never brought the boy to confide in him. This was a capital fault, for the young are naturally ingenuous; so that the acquisition of their confidence is the very first step towards their docility; and, for maintaining parental authority, there is no need to overawe them. "As far as I can judge of my son," says Petrarch, "he has a tolerable understanding; but I am not certain of this, for I do not sufficiently know him. When he is with me he always keeps silence; whether my presence is irksome and confusing to him, or whether shame for his ignorance closes his lips. I suspect it is the latter, for I perceive too clearly his antipathy to letters. I never saw it stronger in any one; he dreads and detests nothing so much as a book; yet he was brought up at Parma, Verona, and Padua. I sometimes direct a few sharp pleasantries at this disposition. 'Take care,' I say, 'lest you should eclipse your neighbour, Virgil.' When I talk in this manner, he looks down and blushes. On this behaviour alone I build my hope. He is modest, and has a docility which renders him susceptible of every impression." This is a melancholy confession, on the part of Petrarch, of his own incompetence to make the most of his son's mind, and a confession the more convincing that it is made unconsciously.

In the summer of 1352, the people of Avignon witnessed the impressive spectacle of the far-famed Tribune Rienzo entering their city, but in a style very different from the pomp of his late processions in Rome. He had now for his attendants only two archers, between whom he walked as a prisoner. It is necessary to say a few words about the circumstances which befell Rienzo after his fall, and which brought him now to the Pope's tribunal at Avignon.

Petrarch says of him at this period, "The Tribune, formerly so powerful and dreaded, but now the most unhappy of men, has been brought hither as a prisoner. I praised and I adored him. I loved his virtue, and I admired his courage. I thought that Rome was about to resume, under him, the empire she formerly held. Ah! had he continued as he began, he would have been praised and admired by the world and by posterity. On entering the city," Petrarch continues, "he inquired if I was there. I knew not whether he hoped for succour from me, or what I could do to serve him. In the process against him they accuse him of nothing criminal. They cannot impute to him having joined with bad men. All that they charge him with is an attempt to give freedom to the republic, and to make Rome the centre of its government. And is this a crime worthy of the wheel or the gibbet? A Roman citizen afflicted to see his country, which is by right the mistress of the world, the slave of the vilest of men!"

Clement was glad to have Rienzo in his power, and ordered him into his presence. Thither the Tribune came, not in the least disconcerted. He denied the accusation of heresy, and insisted that his cause should be re-examined with more equity. The Pope made him no reply, but imprisoned him in a high tower, in which he was chained by the leg to the floor of his apartment. In other respects he was treated mildly, allowed books to read, and supplied with dishes from the Pope's kitchen.

Rienzo begged to be allowed an advocate to defend him; his request was refused. This refusal enraged Petrarch, who wrote, according to De Sade and others, on this occasion, that mysterious letter, which is found in his "Epistles without a title." It is an appeal to the Romans in behalf of their Tribune. I must confess that even the authority of De Sade does not entirely eradicate from my mind a suspicion as to the spuriousness of this inflammatory letter, from the consequences of which Petrarch could hardly have escaped with impunity.

One of the circumstances that detained Petrarch at Avignon was the illness of the Pope, which retarded his decision on several important affairs. Clement VI. was fast approaching to his end, and Petrarch had little hope of his convalescence, at least in the hands of doctors. A message from the Pope produced an imprudent letter from the poet, in which he says, "Holy father! I shudder at the account of your fever; but, believe me, I am not a flatterer. I tremble to see your bed always surrounded with physicians, who are never agreed, because it would be a reproach to the second to think like the first. 'It is not to be doubted,' as Pliny says, 'that physicians, desiring to raise a name by their discoveries, make experiments upon us, and thus barter away our lives. There is no law for punishing their extreme ignorance. They learn their trade at our expense, they make some progress in the art of curing; and they alone are permitted to murder with impunity.' Holy father! consider as your enemies the crowd of physicians who beset you. It is in our age that we behold verified the prediction of the elder Cato, who declared that corruption would be general when the Greeks should have transmitted the sciences to Rome, and, above all, the science of healing. Whole nations have done without this art. The Roman republic, according to Pliny, was without physicians for six hundred years, and was never in a more flourishing condition."

The Pope, a poor dying old man, communicated Petrarch's letter immediately to his physicians, and it kindled in the whole faculty a flame of indignation, worthy of being described by Molière. Petrarch made a general enemy of the physicians, though, of course, the weakest and the worst of them were the first to attack him. One of them told him, "You are a foolhardy man, who, contemning the physicians, have no fear either of the fever or of the malaria." Petrarch replied, "I certainly have no assurance of being free from the attacks of either; but, if I were attacked by either, I should not think of calling in physicians."

His first assailant was one of Clement's own physicians, who loaded him with scurrility in a formal letter. These circumstances brought forth our poet's "Four Books of Invectives against Physicians," a work in which he undoubtedly exposes a great deal of contemporary quackery, but which, at the same time, scarcely leaves the physician-hunter on higher ground than his antagonists.

In the last year of his life, Clement VI. wished to attach our poet permanently to his court by making him his secretary, and Petrarch, after much coy refusal, was at last induced, by the solicitations of his friends, to accept the office. But before he could enter upon it, an objection to his filling it was unexpectedly started. It was discovered that his style was too lofty to suit the humility of the Roman Church. The elevation of Petrarch's style might be obvious, but certainly the humility of the Church was a bright discovery. Petrarch, according to his own account, so far from promising to bring down his magniloquence to a level with church humility, seized the objection as an excuse for declining the secretaryship. He compares his joy on this occasion to that of a prisoner finding the gates of his prison thrown open. He returned to Vaucluse, where he waited impatiently for the autumn, when he meant to return to Italy. He thus describes, in a letter to his dear Simonides, the manner of life which he there led:—

"I make war upon my body, which I regard as my enemy. My eyes, that have made me commit so many follies, are well fixed on a safe object. They look only on a woman who is withered, dark, and sunburnt. Her soul, however, is as white as her complexion is black, and she has the air of being so little conscious of her own appearance, that her homeliness may be said to become her. She passes whole days in the open fields, when the grasshoppers can scarcely endure the sun. Her tanned hide braves the heats of the dog-star, and, in the evening, she arrives as fresh as if she had just risen from bed. She does all the work of my house, besides taking care of her husband and children and attending my guests. She seems occupied with everybody but herself. At night she sleeps on vine-branches; she eats only black bread and roots, and drinks water and vinegar. If you were to give her anything more delicate, she would be the worse for it: such is the force of habit.

"Though I have still two fine suits of clothes, I never wear them. If you saw me, you would take me for a labourer or a shepherd, though I was once so tasteful in my dress. The times are changed; the eyes which I wished to please are now shut; and, perhaps, even if they were opened, they would not *now* have the same empire over me."

In another letter from Vaucluse, he says: "I rise at midnight; I go out at break of day; I study in the fields as in my library; I read, I write, I dream; I struggle against indolence, luxury, and pleasure. I wander all day among the arid mountains, the fresh valleys, and the deep caverns. I walk much on the banks of the Sorgue, where I meet no one to distract me. I recall the past. I deliberate on the future; and, in this contemplation, I find a resource against my solitude." In the same letter he avows that he could accustom himself to any habitation in the world, except Avignon. At this time he was meditating to recross the Alps.

Early in September, 1352, the Cardinal of Boulogne departed for Paris, in order to negotiate a peace between the Kings of France and England. Petrarch went to take his leave of him, and asked if he had any orders for Italy, for which he expected soon to set out. The Cardinal told him that he should be only a month upon his journey, and that he hoped to see him at Avignon on his return. He had, in fact, kind views with regard to Petrarch. He wished to procure for him some good establishment in France, and wrote to him upon his route, "Pray do not depart yet. Wait until I return, or, at least, until I write to you on an important affair that concerns yourself." This letter, which, by the way, evinces that our poet's circumstances were not independent of church promotion, changed the plans of Petrarch, who remained at Avignon nearly the whole of the months of September and October.

During this delay, he heard constant reports of the war that was going on between the Genoese and the Venetians. In the spring of the year 1352, their fleets met in the Propontis, and had a conflict almost unexampled, which lasted during two days and a tempestuous night. The Genoese, upon the whole, had the advantage, and, in revenge for the Greeks having aided the Venetians, they made a league with the Turks. The Pope, who had it earnestly at heart to put a stop to this fatal war, engaged the belligerents to send their ambassadors to Avignon, and there to treat for peace. The ambassadors came; but a whole month was spent in negotiations which ended in nothing. Petrarch in vain employed his eloquence, and the Pope his conciliating talents. In these circumstances, Petrarch wrote a letter to the Genoese government, which does infinite credit to his head and his heart. He used every argument that common sense or humanity could suggest to show the folly of the war, but his arguments were thrown away on spirits too fierce for reasoning.

A few days after writing this letter, as the Cardinal of Boulogne had not kept his word about returning to Avignon, and as he heard no news of him, Petrarch determined to set out for Italy. He accordingly started on the 16th of November, 1352; but scarcely had he left his own house, with all his papers, when he was overtaken by heavy falls of rain. At first he thought of going back immediately; but he changed his purpose, and proceeded as far as Cavaillon, which is two leagues from Vaucluse, in order to take leave of his friend, the Bishop of Cabassole. His good friend was very unwell, but received him with joy, and pressed him to pass the night under his roof. That night and all the next day it rained so heavily that Petrarch, more from fear of his books and papers being damaged than from anxiety about his own health, gave up his Italian journey for the present, and, returning to Vaucluse, spent there the rest of November and the whole of December, 1352.

Early in December, Petrarch heard of the death of Clement VI., and this event gave him occasion for more epistles, both against the Roman court and his enemies, the physicians. Clement's death was ascribed to different causes. Petrarch, of course, imputed it to his doctors. Villani's opinion is the most probable, that he died of a protracted fever. He was buried with great pomp in the church of Nôtre Dame at Avignon; but his remains, after some time, were removed to the abbey of Chaise Dieu, in Auvergne, where his tomb was violated by the Huguenots in 1562. Scandal says that they made a football of his head, and that the Marquis de Courton afterwards converted his skull into a drinking-cup.

It need not surprise us that his Holiness never stood high in the good graces of Petrarch. He was a Limousin, who never loved Italy go much as Gascony, and, in place of re-establishing the holy seat at Rome, he completed the building of the papal palace at Avignon, which his predecessor had begun. These were faults that eclipsed all the good qualities of Clement VI. in the eyes of Petrarch, and, in the sixth of his eclogues, the poet has drawn the character of Clement in odious colours, and, with equal freedom, has described most of the cardinals of his court. Whether there was perfect consistency between this hatred to the Pope and his thinking, as he certainly did for a time, of becoming his secretary, may admit of a doubt. I am not, however, disposed to deny some allowance to Petrarch for his dislike of Clement, who was a voluptuary in private life, and a corrupted ruler of the Church.

Early in May, 1353, Petrarch departed for Italy, and we find him very soon afterwards at the palace of John Visconti of Milan, whom he used to call the greatest man in Italy. This prince, uniting the sacerdotal with the civil power, reigned absolute in Milan. He was master of Lombardy, and made all Italy tremble at his hostility. Yet, in spite of his despotism, John Visconti was a lover of letters, and fond of having literary men at his court. He exercised a cunning influence over our poet, and detained him. Petrarch, knowing that Milan was a troubled city and a stormy court, told the Prince that, being a priest, his vocation did not permit him to live in a princely court, and in the midst of arms. "For that matter," replied the Archbishop, "I am myself an ecclesiastic; I wish to press no employment upon you, but only to request you to remain as an ornament of my court." Petrarch, taken by surprise, had not fortitude to resist his importunities. All that he bargained for was, that he should have a habitation sufficiently distant from the city, and that he should not be obliged to make any change in his ordinary mode of living. The Archbishop was too happy to possess him on these terms.

Petrarch, accordingly, took up his habitation in the western part of the city, near the Vercellina gate, and the church of St. Ambrosio. His house was flanked with two towers, stood behind the city wall, and looked out upon a rich and beautiful country, as far as the Alps, the tops of which, although it was summer, were still covered with snow. Great was the joy of Petrarch when he found himself in a house near the church of that Saint Ambrosio, for whom he had always cherished a peculiar reverence. He himself tells us that he never entered that temple without experiencing rekindled devotion. He visited the statue of the saint, which was niched in one of the walls, and the stone figure seemed to him to breathe, such was the majesty and tranquillity of the sculpture. Near the church arose the chapel, where St. Augustin, after his victory over his refractory passions, was bathed in the sacred fountain of St. Ambrosio, and absolved from penance for his past life.

All this time, whilst Petrarch was so well pleased with his new abode, his friends were astonished, and even grieved, at his fixing himself at Milan. At Avignon, Socrates, Guido Settimo, and the Bishop of Cavaillon, said among themselves, "What! this proud republican, who breathed nothing but independence, who scorned an office in the papal court as a gilded yoke, has gone and thrown himself into the chains of the tyrant of Italy; this misanthrope, who delighted only in the silence of fields, and perpetually praised a secluded life, now inhabits the most bustling of cities!" At Florence, his friends entertained the same sentiments, and wrote to him reproachfully on the subject. "I would wish to be silent," says Boccaccio, "but I cannot hold my peace. My reverence for you would incline me to hold silence, but my indignation obliges me to speak out. How has Silvanus acted?" (Under the name of Silvanus he couches that of Petrarch, in allusion to his love of rural retirement.) "He has forgotten his dignity; he has forgotten all the language he used to hold respecting the state of Italy, his hatred of the Archbishop, and his love of liberty; and he would imprison the Muses in that court. To whom can we now give our faith, when Silvanus, who formerly pronounced the Visconti a cruel tyrant, has now bowed himself to the yoke which he once so boldly condemned? How has the Visconti obtained this truckling, which neither King Robert, nor the Pope, nor the Emperor, could ever obtain? You will say, perhaps, that you have been ill-used by your fellow-citizens, who have withheld from you your paternal property. I disapprove not your just indignation; but Heaven forbid I should believe that, righteously and honestly, any injury, from whomsoever we may receive it, can justify our taking part against our country. It is in vain for you to allege that you have not incited him to war against our country, nor lent him either your arm or advice. How can you be happy with him, whilst you are hearing of the ruins, the conflagrations, the imprisonments, the deaths, and the rapines, that he spreads around him?"

Petrarch's answers to these and other reproaches which his friends sent to him were cold, vague, and unsatisfactory. He denied that he had sacrificed his liberty; and told Boccaccio that, after all, it was less humiliating to be subservient to a single tyrant than to be, as he, Boccaccio, was, subservient to a whole tyrannical people. This was an unwise, implied confession on the part of Petrarch that he was the slave of Visconti. Sismondi may be rather harsh in pronouncing Petrarch to have been all his life a Troubadour; but there is something in his friendship with the Lord of Milan that palliates the accusation. In spite of this severe letter from Boccaccio, it is strange, and yet, methinks, honourable to both, that their friendship was never broken.

Levati, in his *"Viaggi di Petrarca,"* ascribes the poet's settlement at Milan to his desire of accumulating a little money, not for himself, but for his natural children; and in some of Petrarch's letters, subsequent to this period, there are allusions to his own circumstances which give countenance to this suspicion.

However this may be, Petrarch deceived himself if he expected to have long tranquillity in such a court as that of Milan. He was perpetually obliged to visit the Viscontis, and to be present at every feast that they gave to honour the arrival of any illustrious stranger. A more than usually important visitant soon came to Milan, in the person of Cardinal Egidio Albornoz, who arrived at the head of an army, with a view to restore to the Church large portions of its territory which had been seized by some powerful families. The Cardinal entered Milan on the 14th of September, 1353. John Visconti, though far from being delighted at his arrival, gave him an honourable reception, defrayed all the expenses of his numerous retinue, and treated him magnificently. He went out himself to meet him, two miles from the city, accompanied by his nephews and his courtiers, including Petrarch. Our poet joined the suite of Galeazzo Visconti, and rode near him. The Legate and his retinue rode also on horseback. When the two parties met, the dust, that rose in clouds from the feet of the horses, prevented them from discerning each other. Petrarch, who had advanced beyond the rest, found himself, he knew not how, in the midst of the Legate's train, and very near to him. Salutations passed on either side, but with very little speaking, for the dust had dried their throats.

Petrarch made a backward movement, to regain his place among his company. His horse, in backing, slipped with his hind-legs into a ditch on the side of the road, but, by a sort of miracle, the animal kept his fore-feet for some time on the top of the ditch. If he had fallen back, he must have crushed his rider. Petrarch was not afraid, for he was not aware of his danger; but Galeazzo Visconti and his people dismounted to rescue the poet, who escaped without injury.

The Legate treated Petrarch, who little expected it, with the utmost kindness and distinction, and, granting all that he asked for his friends, pressed him to mention something worthy of his own acceptance. Petrarch replied: "When I ask for my friends, is it not the same as for myself? Have I not the highest satisfaction in receiving favours for them? I have long put a rein on my own desires. Of what, then, can I stand in need?"

After the departure of the Legate, Petrarch retired to his *rus in urbe*. In a letter dated thence to his friend the Prior of the Holy Apostles, we find him acknowledging feelings that were far distant from settled contentment. "You have heard," he says, "how much my peace has been disturbed, and my leisure broken in upon, by an importunate crowd and by unforeseen occupations. The Legate has left Milan. He was received at Florence with unbounded applause: as for poor me, I am again in my retreat. I have been long free, happy, and master of my time; but I feel, at present, that liberty and leisure are only for souls of consummate virtue. When we are not of that class of beings, nothing is more dangerous for a heart subject to the passions than to be free, idle, and alone. The snares of voluptuousness are *then* more dangerous, and corrupt thoughts gain an easier entrance—above all, love, that seducing tormentor, from whom I thought that I had now nothing more to fear."

From these expressions we might almost conclude that he had again fallen in love; but if it was so, we have no evidence as to the object of his new passion.

During his half-retirement, Petrarch learned news which disturbed his repose. A courier arrived, one night, bringing an account of the entire destruction of the Genoese fleet, in a naval combat with that of the Venetians, which took place on the

19th of August, 1353, near the island of Sardinia. The letters which the poet had written, in order to conciliate those two republics, had proved as useless as the pacificatory efforts of Clement VI. and his successor, Innocent. Petrarch, who had constantly predicted the eventual success of Genoa, could hardly believe his senses, when he heard of the Genoese being defeated at sea. He wrote a letter of lamentation and astonishment on the subject to his friend Guido Settimo. He saw, as it were, one of the eyes of his country destroying the other. The courier, who brought these tidings to Milan, gave a distressing account of the state of Genoa. There was not a family which had not lost one of its members.

Petrarch passed a whole night in composing a letter to the Genoese, in which he exhorted them, after the example of the Romans, never to despair of the republic. His lecture never reached them. On awakening in the morning, Petrarch learned that the Genoese had lost every spark of their courage, and that the day before they had subscribed the most humiliating concessions in despair.

It has been alleged by some of his biographers that Petrarch suppressed his letter to the Genoese from his fear of the Visconti family. John Visconti had views on Genoa, which was a port so conveniently situated that he naturally coveted the possession of it. He invested it on all sides by land, whilst its other enemies blockaded it by sea; so that the city was reduced to famine. The partizans of John Visconti insinuated to the Genoese that they had no other remedy than to place themselves under the protection of the Prince of Milan. Petrarch was not ignorant of the Visconti's views; and it has been, therefore, suspected that he kept back his exhortatory epistle from his apprehension, that if he had despatched it, John Visconti would have made it the last epistle of his life. The morning after writing it, he found that Genoa had signed a treaty of almost abject submission; after which his exhortation would have been only an insult to the vanquished.

The Genoese were not long in deliberating on the measures which they were to take. In a few days their deputies arrived at Milan, imploring the aid and protection of John Visconti, as well as offering him the republic of Genoa and all that belonged to it. After some conferences, the articles of the treaty were signed; and the Lord of Milan accepted with pleasure the possession that was offered to him.

Petrarch, as a counsellor of Milan, attended these conferences, and condoled with the deputies from Genoa; though we cannot suppose that he approved, in his heart, of the desperate submission of the Genoese in thus throwing themselves into the arms of the tyrant of Italy, who had been so long anxious either to invade them in open quarrel, or to enter their States upon a more amicable pretext. John Visconti immediately took possession of the city of Genoa; and, after having deposed the doge and senate, took into his own hands the reins of government.

Albenga, Coast of Genoa. Artist: James Duffield Harding (1797-1863).

Weary of Milan, Petrarch betook himself to the country, and made a temporary residence at the castle of St. Columba, which was now a monastery. This mansion was built in 1164, by the celebrated Frederick Barbarossa. It now belonged to the Carthusian monks of Pavia. Petrarch has given a beautiful description of this edifice, and of the magnificent view which it commands.

Whilst he was enjoying this glorious scenery, he received a letter from Socrates, informing him that he had gone to Vaucluse in company with Guido Settimo, whose intention to accompany Petrarch in his journey to Italy had been prevented by a fit of illness. Petrarch, when he heard of this visit, wrote to express his happiness at their thus honouring his habitation, at the same time lamenting that he was not one of their party. "Repair," he said, "often to the same retreat. Make use of my books, which deplore the absence of their owner, and the death of their keeper" (he alluded to his old servant). "My country-house is the temple of peace, and the home of repose."

From the contents of his letter, on this occasion, it is obvious that he had not yet found any spot in Italy where he could determine on fixing himself permanently; otherwise he would not have left his books behind him.

When he wrote about his books, he was little aware of the danger that was impending over them. On Christmas day a troop of robbers, who had for some time infested the neighbourhood of Vaucluse, set fire to the poet's house, after having taken away everything that they could carry off. An ancient vault stopped the conflagration, and saved the mansion from being entirely consumed by the flames. Luckily, the person to whose care he had left his house—the son of the worthy rustic, lately deceased—having a presentiment of the robbery, had conveyed to the castle a great many books which Petrarch left behind him; and the robbers, believing that there were persons in the castle to defend it, had not the courage to make an attack.

As Petrarch grew old, we do not find him improve in consistency. In his letter, dated the 21st of October, 1353, it is evident that he had a return of his hankering after Vaucluse. He accordingly wrote to his friends, requesting that they would procure him an establishment in the Comtat. Socrates, upon this, immediately communicated with the Bishop of Cavaillon, who did all that he could to obtain for the poet the object of his wish. It appears that the Bishop endeavoured to get for him a good benefice in his own diocese. The thing was never accomplished. Without doubt, the enemies, whom he had excited by writing freely about the Church, and who were very numerous at Avignon, frustrated his wishes.

After some time Petrarch received a letter from the Emperor Charles IV. in answer to one which the poet had expedited to him about three years before. Our poet, of course, did not fail to acknowledge his Imperial Majesty's late-coming letter. He commences his reply with a piece of pleasantry: "I see very well," he says, "that it is as difficult for your Imperial Majesty's despatches and couriers to cross the Alps, as it is for your person and legions." He wonders that the Emperor had not followed his advice, and hastened into Italy, to take possession of the empire. "What consoles me," he adds, "is, that if you do not adopt my sentiments, you at least approve of my zeal; and that is the greatest recompense I could receive." He argues the question with the Emperor with great force and eloquence; and, to be sure, there never was a fairer opportunity for Charles IV. to enter Italy. The reasons which his Imperial Majesty alleges, for waiting a little time to watch the course of events, display a timid and wavering mind.

A curious part of his letter is that in which he mentions Rienzo. "Lately," he says, "we have seen at Rome, suddenly elevated to supreme power, a man who was neither king, nor consul, nor patrician, and who was hardly known as a Roman citizen. Although he was not distinguished by his ancestry, yet he dared to declare himself the restorer of public liberty. What title more brilliant for an obscure man! Tuscany immediately submitted to him. All Italy followed her example; and Europe and the whole world were in one movement. We have seen the event; it is not a doubtful tale of history. Already, under the reign of the Tribune, justice, peace, good faith, and security, were restored, and we saw vestiges of the golden age appearing once more. In the moment of his most brilliant success, he chose to submit to others. I blame nobody. I wish neither to acquit nor to condemn; but I know what I ought to think.

That man had only the title of Tribune. Now, if the name of Tribune could produce such an effect, what might not the title of Cæsar produce!"

Charles did not enter Italy until a year after the date of our poet's epistle; and it is likely that the increasing power of John Visconti made a far deeper impression on his irresolute mind than all the rhetoric of Petrarch. Undoubtedly, the petty lords of Italy were fearful of the vipers of Milan. It was thus that they denominated the Visconti family, in allusion to their coat of arms, which represented an immense serpent swallowing a child, though the device was not their own, but borrowed from a standard which they had taken from the Saracens. The submission of Genoa alarmed the whole of Italy. The Venetians took measures to form a league against the Visconti; and the Princes of Padua, Modena, Mantua, and Verona joined it, and the confederated lords sent a deputation to the Emperor, to beg that he would support them; and they proposed that he should enter Italy at their expense. The opportunity was too good to be lost; and the Emperor promised to do all that they wished. This league gave great trouble to John Visconti. In order to appease the threatening storm, he immediately proposed to the Emperor that he should come to Milan and receive the iron crown; while he himself, by an embassy from Milan, would endeavour to restore peace between the Venetians and the Genoese.

Petrarch appeared to John Visconti the person most likely to succeed in this negotiation, by his eloquence, and by his intimacy with Andrea Dandolo, who governed the republic of Venice. The poet now wished for repose, and journeys began to fatigue him; but the Visconti knew so well how to flatter and manage him, that he could not resist the proposal.

At the commencement of the year 1354, before he departed for Venice, Petrarch received a present, which gave him no small delight. It was a Greek Homer, sent to him by Nichola Sigeros, Prætor of Romagna. Petrarch wrote a long letter of thanks to Sigeros, in which there is a remarkable confession of the small progress which he had made in the Greek language, though at the same time he begs his friend Sigeros to send him copies of Hesiod and Euripides.

A few days afterwards he set out to Venice. He was the chief of the embassy. He went with confidence, flattering himself that he should find the Venetians more tractable and disposed to peace, both from their fear of John Visconti, and from some checks which their fleet had experienced, since their victory off Sardinia. But he was unpleasantly astonished to find the Venetians more exasperated than humbled by their recent losses, and by the union of the Lord of Milan with the Genoese. All his eloquence could not bring them to accept the proposals he had to offer. Petrarch completely failed in his negotiation, and, after passing a month at Venice, he returned to Milan full of chagrin.

Two circumstances seem to have contributed to render the Venetians intractable. The princes with whom they were leagued had taken into their pay the mercenary troops of Count Lando, which composed a very formidable force; and further, the Emperor promised to appear very soon in Italy at the head of an army.

Some months afterwards, Petrarch wrote to the Doge of Venice, saying, that he saw with grief that the hearts of the Venetians were shut against wise counsels, and he then praises John Visconti as a lover of peace and humanity.

After a considerable interval, Andrea Dandolo answered our poet's letter, and was very sarcastic upon him for his eulogy on John Visconti. At this moment, Visconti was arming the Genoese fleet, the command of which he gave to Paganino Doria, the admiral who had beaten the Venetians in the Propontis. Doria set sail with thirty-three vessels, entered the Adriatic, sacked and pillaged some towns, and did much damage on the Venetian coast. The news of this descent spread consternation in Venice. It was believed that the Genoese fleet were in the roads; and the Doge took all possible precautions to secure the safety of the State.

But Dandolo's health gave way at this crisis, vexed as he was to see the maiden city so humbled in her pride. His constitution rapidly declined, and he died the 8th of September, 1354. He was extremely popular among the Venetians. Petrarch, in a letter written shortly after his death, says of him: "He was a virtuous man, upright, full of love and zeal for his republic; learned, eloquent, wise, and affable. He had only one fault, to wit, that he loved war too much. From this error he judged of a cause by its event. The luckiest cause always appeared to him the most just, which made him often repeat what Scipio Africanus said, and what Lucan makes Cæsar repeat: 'Hæc acies victum factura nocentem.'"

If Dandolo had lived a little longer, and continued his ethical theory of judging a cause by its success, he would have had a hint, from the disasters of Venice, that his own cause was not the most righteous. The Genoese, having surprised the Venetians off the island of Sapienza, obtained one of the completest victories on record. All the Venetian vessels, with the exception of one that escaped, were taken, together with their admiral. It is believed that, if the victors had gone immediately to Venice, they might have taken the city, which was defenceless, and in a state of consternation; but the Genoese preferred returning home to announce their triumph, and to partake in the public joy. About the time of the Doge's death, another important public event took place in the death of John Visconti. He had a carbuncle upon his forehead, just above the eyebrows, which he imprudently caused to be cut; and, on the very day of the operation, October 4th, 1354, he expired so suddenly as not to have time to receive the sacrament.

John Visconti had three nephews, Matteo, Galeazzo, and Barnabo. They were his heirs, and took possession of his dominions in common, a few days after his death, without any dispute among themselves. The day for their inauguration was fixed, such was the superstition of the times, by an astrologer; and on that day Petrarch was commissioned to make to the assembled people an address suited to the ceremony. He was still in the midst of his harangue, when the astrologer declared with a loud voice that the moment for the ceremony was come, and that it would be dangerous to let it pass. Petrarch, heartily as he despised the false science, immediately stopped his discourse. The astrologer, somewhat disconcerted, replied that there was still a little time, and that the orator might continue to speak. Petrarch answered that he had nothing more to say. Whilst some laughed, and others were indignant at the interruption, the astrologer exclaimed "that the happy moment was come;" on which an old officer carried three white stakes, like the palisades of a town, and gave one to each of the brothers; and the ceremony was thus concluded.

The countries which the three brothers shared amongst them comprehended not only what was commonly called the Duchy, before the King of Sardinia acquired a great part of it, but the territories of Parma, Piacenza, Bologna, Lodi, Bobbio, Pontremoli, and many other places.

There was an entire dissimilarity among the brothers. Matteo hated business, and was addicted to the grossest debaucheries. Barnabo was a monster of tyranny and cruelty. Petrarch, nevertheless, condescended to be godfather to one of Barnabo's sons, and presented the child with a gilt cup. He also composed a Latin poem, on the occasion of his godson being christened by the name of Marco, in which he passes in review all the great men who had borne that name.

Galeazzo was very different from his brothers. He had much kindliness of disposition. One of his greatest pleasures was his intercourse with men of letters. He almost worshipped Petrarch, and it was his influence that induced the poet to settle at Milan. Unlike as they were in dispositions, the brothers, nevertheless, felt how important it was that they should be united, in order to protect themselves against the league which threatened them; and, at first, they lived in the greatest harmony. Barnabo, the most warlike, was charged with whatever concerned the military. Business of every other kind devolved on Galeazzo. Matteo, as the eldest, presided over all; but, conscious of his incapacity, he took little share in the deliberations of his brothers. Nothing important was done without consulting Petrarch; and this flattering confidence rendered Milan as agreeable to him as any residence could be, consistently with his love of change.

The deaths of the Doge of Venice and of the Lord of Milan were soon followed by another, which, if it had happened some years earlier, would have strongly affected Petrarch. This was the tragic end of Rienzo. Our poet's opinion of this extraordinary man had been changed by his later conduct, and he now took but a comparatively feeble interest in him. Under the pontificate of Clement VI., the ex-Tribune, after his fall, had been consigned to a prison at Avignon. Innocent, the succeeding Pope, thought differently of him from his predecessor, and sent the Cardinal Albornoz into Italy, with an order to establish him at Rome, and to confide the government of the city to him under the title of senator. The Cardinal obeyed the injunction; but after a brief and inglorious struggle with the faction of the Colonnas, Rienzo perished in a popular sedition on the 8th of October, 1354.

War was now raging between the States of the Venetian League and Milan, united with Genoa, when a new actor was brought upon the scene. The Emperor, who had been solicited by one half of Italy to enter the kingdom, but who hesitated from dread of the Lord of Milan, was evidently induced by the intelligence of John Visconti's death to accept this invitation. In October, 1354, his Imperial Majesty entered Italy, with no show of martial preparation, being attended by only three hundred horsemen. On the 10th of November he arrived at Mantua, where he was received as sovereign. There he stopped for some time, before he pursued his route to Rome.

The moment Petrarch heard of his arrival, he wrote to his Imperial Majesty in transports of joy. "You are no longer," he said, "king of Bohemia. I behold in you the king of the world, the Roman emperor, the true Cæsar." The Emperor received this letter at Mantua, and in a few days sent Sacromore de Pomieres, one of his squires, to invite Petrarch to come and meet him, expressing the utmost eagerness to see him. Petrarch could not resist so flattering an invitation; he was not to be deterred even by the unprecedented severity of the frost, and departed from Milan on the 9th of December; but, with all the speed that he could make, was not able to reach Mantua till the 12th.

The Emperor thanked him for having come to him in such dreadful weather, the like of which he had scarcely ever felt, even in Germany. "The Emperor," says Petrarch, "received me in a manner that partook neither of imperial haughtiness nor of German etiquette. We passed sometimes whole days together, from morning to night, in conversation, as if his Majesty had had nothing else to do. He spoke to me about my works, and expressed a great desire to see them, particularly my 'Treatise on Illustrious Men.' I told him that I had not yet put my last hand to it, and that, before I could do so, I required to have leisure and repose. He gave me to understand that he should be very glad to see it appear under his own patronage, that is to say, dedicated to himself. I said to him, with that freedom of speech which Nature has given me, and which years have fortified, 'Great prince, for this purpose, nothing more is necessary than, virtue on your part, and leisure on mine.' He asked me to explain myself. I said, 'I must have time for a work of this nature, in which I propose to include great things in a small space. On your part, labour to deserve that your name should appear at the head of my book. For this end, it is not enough that you wear a crown; your virtues and great actions must place you among the great men whose portraits I have delineated. Live in such a manner, that, after reading the lives of your illustrious predecessors, you may feel assured that your own life shall deserve to be read by posterity.'

"The Emperor showed by a smile that my liberty had not displeased him, I seized this opportunity of presenting him with some imperial medals, in gold and in silver, and gave him a short sketch of the lives of those worthies whose images they bore. He seemed to listen to me with pleasure, and, graciously accepting the medals, declared that he never had received a more agreeable present.

"I should never end if I were to relate to you all the conversations which I held with this prince. He desired me one day to relate the history of my life to him. I declined to do so at first; but he would take no refusal, and I obeyed him. He heard me with attention, and, if I omitted any circumstances from forgetfulness or the fear of being wearisome, he brought them back to my memory. He then asked me what were my projects for the future, and my plans for the rest of my life. 'My intentions are good,' I replied to him, 'but a bad habit, which I cannot conquer, masters my better will, and I resemble a sea beaten by two opposite winds,' 'I can understand that,' he said; 'but I wish to know what is the kind of life that would most decidedly please you?' 'A secluded life,' I replied to him, without hesitation. 'If I could, I should go and seek for such a life at its fountain-head; that is, among the woods and mountains, as I have already done. If I could not go so far to find it, I should seek to enjoy it in the midst of cities.'

"The Emperor differed from me totally as to the benefits of a solitary life. I told him that I had composed a treatise on the subject. 'I know that,' said the Emperor; 'and if I ever find your book, I shall throw it into the fire.' 'And,' I replied, 'I shall take care that it never falls into your hands.' On this subject we had long and frequent disputes, always seasoned with pleasantry. I must confess that the Emperor combated my system on a solitary life with surprising energy."

Petrarch remained eight days with the King of Bohemia, at Mantua, where he was witness to all his negotiations with the Lords of the league of Lombardy, who came to confer with his Imperial Majesty, in that city, or sent thither their ambassadors. The Emperor, above all things, wished to ascertain the strength of this confederation; how much each principality would contribute, and how much might be the sum total of the whole contribution. The result of this inquiry was, that the forces of the united confederates were not sufficient to make head against the

Visconti, who had thirty thousand well-disciplined men. The Emperor, therefore, decided that it was absolutely necessary to conclude a peace. This prince, pacific and without ambition, had, indeed, come into Italy with this intention; and was only anxious to obtain two crowns without drawing a sword. He saw, therefore, with satisfaction that there was no power in Italy to protract hostilities by strengthening the coalition.

He found difficulties, however, in the settlement of a general peace. The Viscontis felt their superiority; and the Genoese, proud of a victory which they had obtained over the Venetians, insisted on hard terms. The Emperor, more intent upon his personal interests than the good of Italy, merely negotiated a truce between the belligerents. He prevailed upon the confederates to disband the company of Count Lando, which cost much and effected little. It cannot be doubted that Petrarch had considerable influence in producing this dismissal, as he always held those troops of mercenaries in abhorrence. The truce being signed, his Imperial Majesty had no further occupation than to negotiate a particular agreement with the Viscontis, who had sent the chief men of Milan, with presents, to conclude a treaty with him. No one appeared more fit than Petrarch to manage this negotiation, and it was universally expected that it should be entrusted to him; but particular reasons, which Petrarch has not thought proper to record, opposed the desires of the Lords of Milan and the public wishes.

The negotiation, nevertheless, was in itself a very easy one. The Emperor, on the one hand, had no wish to make war for the sake of being crowned at Monza. On the other hand, the Viscontis were afraid of seeing the league of their enemies fortified by imperial power. They took advantage of the desire which they observed in Charles to receive this crown without a struggle. They promised not to oppose his coronation, and even to give 50,000 florins for the expense of the ceremony; but they required that he should not enter the city of Milan, and that the troops in his suite should be disarmed.

To these humiliating terms Charles subscribed. The affair was completed during the few days that Petrarch spent at Mantua. The Emperor strongly wished that he should be present at the signature of the treaty; and, in fact, though he was not one of the envoys from Milan, the success of the negotiation was generally attributed to him. A rumour to this effect reached even Avignon, where Lælius then was. He wrote to Petrarch to compliment him on the subject. The poet, in his answer, declines an honour that was not due to him.

After the signature of the treaty, Petrarch departed for Milan, where he arrived on Christmas eve, 1354. He there found four letters from Zanobi di Strata, from whom he had not had news for two years. Curious persons had intercepted their letters to each other. Petrarch often complains of this nuisance, which was common at the time.

The Emperor set out from Mantua after the festivities of Christmas. On arriving at the gates of Milan, he was invited to enter by the Viscontis; but Charles declined their invitation, saying, that he would keep the promise which he had pledged. The Viscontis told him politely that they asked his entrance as a favour, and that the precaution respecting his troops by no means extended to his personal presence, which they should always consider an honour. The Emperor entered Milan on the 4th of January, 1355. He was received with the sound of drums, trumpets, and other instruments, that made such a din as to resemble thunder. "His entry," says Villani, "had the air of a tempest rather than of a festivity." Meanwhile the gates of Milan were shut and strictly guarded. Shortly after his arrival, the three brothers came to tender their homage, declaring that they held of the Holy Empire all that they possessed, and that they would never employ their possessions but for his service.

Next day the three brothers, wishing to give the Emperor a high idea of their power and forces, held a grand review of their troops, horse and foot; to which, in order to swell the number, they added companies of the burgesses, well mounted, and magnificently dressed; and they detained his poor Majesty at a window, by way of amusing him, all the time they were making this display of their power. Whilst the troops were defiling, they bade him look upon the six thousand cavalry and ten thousand infantry, which they kept in their pay for his service, adding that their fortresses and castles were well furnished and garrisoned. This spectacle was anything but amusing to the Emperor; but he put a good countenance on the matter, and appeared cheerful and serene. Petrarch scarcely ever quitted his side; and the Prince conversed with him whenever he could snatch time from business, and from the rigid ceremonials that were imposed on him.

On the 6th of January, the festival of Epiphany, Charles received at Milan the iron crown, in the church of St. Ambrosio, from the hands of Robert Visconti, Archbishop of Milan. They gave the Emperor fifty thousand florins in gold, two hundred beautiful horses, covered with cloth bordered with ermine, and six hundred horsemen to escort him to Rome.

The Emperor, who regarded Milan only as a fine large prison, got out of it as soon as he could. Petrarch accompanied him as far as five miles beyond Pìacenza, but refused to comply with the Emperor's solicitations to continue with him as far as Rome.

The Emperor departed from Sienna the 28th of March, with the Empress and all his suite. On the 2nd of April he arrived at Rome. During the next two days he visited the churches in pilgrim's attire. On Sunday, which was Easter day, he was crowned, along with his Empress; and, on this occasion, he confirmed all the privileges of the Roman Church, and all the promises that he had made to the Popes Clement VI. and Innocent VI. One of those promises was, that he should not enter Rome except upon the day of his coronation, and that he should not sleep in the city. He kept his word most scrupulously. After leaving the church of St. Peter, he went with a grand retinue to St. John's di Latrana, where he dined, and, in the evening, under pretext of a hunting-party, he went and slept at St. Lorenzo, beyond the walls.

The Emperor arrived at Sienna on the 29th of April. He had there many conferences with the Cardinal Albornoz, to whom he promised troops for the purpose of reducing the tyrants with whom the Legate was at war. His Majesty then went to Pisa, where, on the 21st of May, 1355, a sedition broke out against him, which nearly cost him his life. He left Tuscany without delay, with his Empress and his whole suite, to return to Germany, where he arrived early in June. Many were the affronts he met with on his route, and he recrossed the Alps, as Villani says, "with his dignity humbled, though with his purse well filled."

Lælius, who had accompanied the Emperor as far as Cremona, quitted him at that place, and went to Milan, where he delivered to Petrarch the Prince's valedictory compliments. Petrarch's indignation, at his dastardly flight vented itself in a letter to his Imperial Majesty himself, so full of unmeasured rebuke, that it is believed it was never sent.

Shortly after the departure of the Emperor, Petrarch had the satisfaction of hearing, in his own church of St. Ambrosio, the publication of a peace between the Venetians and Genoese. It was concluded at Milan by the mediation of the Visconti, entirely to the advantage of the Genoese, to whom their victory gained in the gulf of Sapienza had given an irresistible superiority. It cost the Venetians two hundred thousand florins. Whilst the treaty of peace was proceeding, Venice witnessed the sad and strange spectacle of Marino Faliero, her venerable Doge, four-score years old, being dragged to a public execution. Some obscurity still hangs over the true history of this affair. Petrarch himself seems to have understood it but imperfectly, though, from his personal acquaintance with Faliero, and his humane indignation at seeing an old man whom he believed to be innocent, hurled from his seat of power, stripped of his ducal robes, and beheaded like the meanest felon, he inveighs against his execution as a public murder, in his letter on the subject to Guido Settimo.

Petrarch, since his establishment at Milan, had thought it his duty to bring thither his son John, that he might watch over his education. John was at this time eighteen years of age, and was studying at Verona.

The September of 1355 was a critical month for our poet. It was then that the tertian ague commonly attacked him, and this year it obliged him to pass a whole month in bed. He was just beginning to be convalescent, when, on the 9th of September, 1355, a friar, from the kingdom of Naples, entered his chamber, and gave him a letter from Barbato di Salmone. This was a great joy to him, and tended to promote the recovery of his health. Their correspondence had been for a long time interrupted by the wars, and the unsafe state of the public roads. This letter was full of enthusiasm and affection, and was addressed to *Francis Petrarch, the king of poets.* The friar had told Barbato that this title was given to Petrarch over all Italy. Our poet in his answer affected to refuse it with displeasure as far beyond his deserts. "There are only two king-poets," he says, "the one in Greece, the other in Italy. The old bard of Mæonia occupies the former kingdom, the shepherd of Mantua is in possession of the latter. As for me, I can only reign in my transalpine solitude and on the banks of the Sorgue."

Petrarch continued rather languid during autumn, but his health was re-established before the winter.

Early in the year 1356, whilst war was raging between Milan and the Lombard and Ligurian league, a report was spread that the King of Hungary had formed a league with the Emperor and the Duke of Austria, to invade Italy. The Italians in alarm sent ambassadors to the King of Hungary, who declared that he had no hostile intentions, except against the Venetians, as they had robbed him of part of Sclavonia. This declaration calmed the other princes, but not the Viscontis, who knew that the Emperor would never forget the manner in which they had treated him. They thought that it would be politic to send an ambassador to Charles, in order to justify themselves before him, or rather to penetrate into his designs, and no person seemed to be more fit for this commission than Petrarch. Our poet had no great desire to journey into the north, but a charge so agreeable and flattering made him overlook the fatigue of travelling. He wrote thus to Simonides on the day before his departure: —"They are sending me to the north, at the time when I am sighing for solitude and repose. But man was made for toil: the charge imposed on me does not displease me, and I shall be recompensed for my fatigue if I succeed in the object of my mission. The Lord of Liguria sends me to treat with the Emperor. After having conferred with him on public affairs, I reckon on being able to treat with him respecting my own, and be my own ambassador. I have reproached this prince by letter with his shameful flight from our country. I shall make him the same reproaches, face to face, and *vivâ voce*. In thus using *my own* liberty and his patience, I shall avenge at once Italy, the empire, and my own person. At my return I shall bury myself in a solitude so profound that toil and envy will not be able to find me out. Yet what folly! Can I flatter myself to find any place where envy cannot penetrate?"

Milan Cathedral.

Next day he departed with Sacromoro di Pomieres, whose company was a great solace to him. They arrived at Basle, where the Emperor was expected; but they waited in vain for him a whole month. "This prince," says Petrarch, "finishes nothing; one must go and seek him in the depths of barbarism." It was fortunate for him that he stayed no longer, for, a few days after he took leave of Basle, the city was almost wholly destroyed by an earthquake.

Petrarch arrived at Prague in Bohemia towards the end of July, 1356. He found the Emperor wholly occupied with that famous Golden Bull, the provisions of which he settled with the States, at the diet of Nuremberg, and which he solemnly promulgated at another grand diet held at Christmas, in the same year. This Magna Charta of the Germanic constitution continued to be the fundamental law of the empire till its dissolution.

Petrarch made but a short stay at Prague, notwithstanding his Majesty's wish to detain him. The Emperor, though sorely exasperated against the Visconti, had no thoughts of carrying war into Italy. His affairs in Germany employed him sufficiently, besides the embellishment of the city of Prague. At the Bohemian court our poet renewed a very amicable acquaintance with two accomplished prelates, Ernest, Archbishop of Pardowitz, and John Oczkow, Bishop of Olmütz. Of these churchmen he speaks in the warmest terms, and he afterwards corresponded with them. We find him returned to Milan, and writing to Simonides on the 20th of September.

Some days after Petrarch's return from Germany, a courier arrived at Milan with news of the battle of Poitiers, in which eighty thousand French were defeated by thirty thousand Englishmen, and in which King John of France was made prisoner.[13] Petrarch was requested by Galeazzo Visconti on this occasion to write for him two condoling letters, one to Charles the Dauphin, and another to the Cardinal of Boulogne. Petrarch was thunderstruck at the calamity of King John, of whom he had an exalted idea. "It is a thing," he says, "incredible, unheard-of, and unexampled in history, that an invincible hero, the greatest king that ever lived, should have been conquered and made captive by an enemy so inferior."

On this great event, our poet composed an allegorical eclogue, in which the King of France, under the name of Pan, and the King of England, under that of Articus, heartily abuse each other. The city of Avignon is brought in with the designation of Faustula. England reproaches the Pope with his partiality for the King of France, to whom he had granted the tithes of his kingdom, by which means he was enabled to levy an army. Articus thus apostrophizes Faustula:—

> Ah meretrix oblique tuens, ait Articus illi—
> Immemorem sponsæ cupidus quam mungit adulter!
> Hæc tua tota fides, sic sic aliena ministras!
> Erubuit nihil ausa palam, nisi mollia pacis
> Verba, sed assuetis noctem complexibus egit—

> Ah, harlot! squinting with lascivious brows
> Upon a hapless wife's adulterous spouse,
> Is this thy faith, to waste another's wealth.
> The guilty fruit of perfidy and stealth!
> She durst not be my foe in open light.
> But in my foe's embraces spent the night.

Meanwhile, Marquard, Bishop of Augsburg, vicar of the Emperor in Italy, having put himself at the head of the Lombard league against the Viscontis, entered their territories with the German troops, and was committing great devastations. But the brothers of Milan turned out, beat the Bishop, and took him prisoner. It is evident, from these hostilities of the Emperor's vicar against the Viscontis, that Petrarch's embassy to Prague had not had the desired success. The Emperor, it is true, plainly told him that he had no thoughts of invading Italy in person. And this was true; but there is no doubt that he abetted and secretly supported the enemies of the Milan chiefs. Powerful as the Visconti were, their numerous enemies pressed them hard; and, with war on all sides, Milan was in a critical situation. But Petrarch, whilst war was at the very gates, continued retouching his Italian poetry.

At the commencement of this year, 1356, he received a letter from Avignon, which Socrates, Lælius, and Guido Settimo had jointly written to him. They dwelt all three in the same house, and lived in the most social union. Petrarch made them a short reply, in which he said, "Little did I think that I should ever envy those who inhabit Babylon. Nevertheless, I wish that I were with you in that house of yours, inaccessible to the pestilent air of the infamous city. I regard it as an elysium in the midst of Avernus."

At this time, Petrarch received a diploma that was sent to him by John, Bishop of Olmütz, Chancellor of the Empire, in which diploma the Emperor created him a count palatine, and conferred upon him the rights and privileges attached to this dignity. These, according to the French abridger of the History of Germany, consisted in creating doctors and notaries, in legitimatizing the bastards of citizens, in crowning poets, in giving dispensations with respect to age, and in other things. To this diploma sent to Petrarch was attached a bull, or capsule of gold. On one side was the impression of the Emperor, seated on his throne, with an eagle and lion beside him; on the other was the city of Rome, with its temples and walls. The Emperor had added to this dignity privileges which he granted to very few, and the Chancellor, in his communication, used very flattering terms. Petrarch says, in his letter of thanks, "I am exceedingly grateful for the signal distinction which the Emperor has graciously vouchsafed to me, and for the obliging terms with which you have seasoned the communication. I have never sought in vain for anything from his Imperial Majesty and yourself. But I wish not for your gold."

In the summer of 1357, Petrarch, wishing to screen himself from the excessive heat, took up his abode for a time on the banks of the Adda at Garignano, a village three miles distant from Milan, of which he gives a charming description. "The village," he says, "stands on a slight elevation in the midst of a plain, surrounded on all sides by springs and streams, not rapid and noisy like those of Vaucluse, but clear and modest. They wind in such a manner, that you know not either whither they are going, or whence they have come. As if to imitate the dances of the nymphs, they approach, they retire, they unite, and they separate alternately. At last, after having formed a kind of labyrinth, they all meet, and pour themselves into the same reservoir." John Visconti had chosen this situation whereon to build a Carthusian monastery. This was what tempted Petrarch to found here a little establishment. He wished at first to live within the walls of the monastery, and the Carthusians made him welcome to do so; but he could not dispense with servants and horses, and he feared that the drunkenness of the former might trouble the silence of the sacred retreat. He therefore hired a house in the neighbourhood of the holy brothers, to whom he repaired at all hours of the day. He called this house his Linterno, in memory of Scipio Africanus, whose country-house bore that name. The peasants, hearing him call the domicile *Linterno*, corrupted the word into *Inferno*, and, from this mispronunciation, the place was often jocularly called by that name.

Petrarch was scarcely settled in this agreeable solitude, when he received a letter from his friend Settimo, asking him for an exact and circumstantial detail of his circumstances and mode of living, of his plans and occupations, of his son John, &c. His answer was prompt, and is not uninteresting. "The course of my life," he says, "has always been uniform ever since the frost of age has quenched the ardour of my youth, and particularly that fatal flame which so long tormented me. But what do I say?" he continues; "it is a celestial dew which has produced this extinction. Though I have often changed my place of abode, I have always led nearly the same kind of life. What it is, none knows better than yourself. I once lived beside you for two years. Call to mind how I was then occupied, and you will know my present occupations. You understand me so well that you ought to be able to guess, not only what I am doing, but what I am dreaming.

"Like a traveller, I am quickening my steps in proportion as I approach the term of my course. I read and write night and day; the one occupation refreshes me from the fatigue of the other These are my employments—these are my pleasures. My tasks increase upon my hands; one begets another; and I am dismayed when I look at what I have undertaken to accomplish in so short a space as the remainder of my life. * * * My health is good; my body is so robust that neither ripe years, nor grave occupations, nor abstinence, nor penance, can totally subdue that *kicking ass* on whom I am constantly making war. I count upon the grace of Heaven, without which I should infallibly fall, as I fell in other times. All my reliance is on Christ. With regard to my fortune, I am exactly in a just mediocrity, equally distant from the two extremes * * * *

"I inhabit a retired corner of the city towards the west. Their ancient devotion attracts the people every Sunday to the church of St. Ambrosio, near which I dwell. During the rest of the week, this quarter is a desert.

"Fortune has changed nothing in my nourishment, or my hours of sleep, except that I retrench as much as possible from indulgence in either. I lie in bed for no other purpose than to sleep, unless I am ill. I hasten from bed as soon as I am awake, and pass into my library. This takes place about the middle of the night, save when the nights are shortest. I grant to Nature nothing but what she imperatively demands, and which it is impossible to refuse her.

"Though I have always loved solitude and silence, I am a great gossip with my friends, which arises, perhaps, from my seeing them but rarely. I atone for this loquacity by a year of taciturnity. I mutely recall my parted friends by correspondence. I resemble that class of people of whom Seneca speaks, who seize life in detail, and not by the gross. The moment I feel the approach of summer, I take a country-house a league distant from town, where the air is extremely pure. In such a place I am at present, and here I lead my wonted life, more free than ever from the wearisomeness of the city. I have abundance of everything; the peasants vie with each other in bringing me fruit, fish, ducks, and all sorts of game. There is a beautiful Carthusian monastery in my neighbourhood, where, at all hours of the day, I find the innocent pleasures which religion offers. In this sweet retreat I feel no want but that of my ancient friends. In these I was once rich; but death has taken away some of them, and absence robs me of the remainder. Though my imagination represents them, still I am not the less desirous of their real presence. There would remain but few things for me to desire, if fortune would restore to me but two friends, such as you and Socrates. I confess that I flattered myself a long time to have had you both with me. But, if you persist in your rigour, I must console myself with the company of my religionists. Their conversation, it is true, is neither witty nor profound, but it is simple and pious. Those good priests will be of great service to me both in life and death. I think I have now said enough about myself, and, perhaps, more than enough. You ask me about the state of my fortune, and you wish to know whether you may believe the rumours that are abroad about my riches. It is true that my income is increased; but so, also, proportionably, is my outlay. I am, as I have always been, neither rich nor poor. Riches, they say, make men poor by multiplying their wants and desires; for my part, I feel the contrary; the more I have the less I desire. Yet, I suppose, if I possessed great riches, they would have the same effect upon me as upon other people.

"You ask news about my son. I know not very well what to say concerning him. His manners are gentle, and the flower of his youth holds out a promise, though what fruit it may produce I know not. I think I may flatter myself that he will be an honest man. He has talent; but what avails talent without study! He flies from a book as he would from a serpent. Persuasions, caresses, and threats are all thrown away upon him as incitements to study. I have nothing wherewith to reproach myself; and I shall be satisfied if he turns out an honest man, as I hope he will. Themistocles used to say that he liked a man without letters better than letters without a man."

In the month of August, 1357, Petrarch received a letter from Benintendi, the Chancellor of Venice, requesting him to send a dozen elegiac verses to be engraved on the tomb of Andrea Dandolo. The children of the Doge had an ardent wish that our poet should grant them this testimony of his friendship for their father. Petrarch could not refuse the request, and composed fourteen verses, which contain a sketch of the great actions of Dandolo. But they were verses of command, which the poet made in despite of the Muses and of himself.

In the following year, 1358, Petrarch was almost entirely occupied with his treatise, entitled, "De Remediis utriusque Fortunæ," (A Remedy against either extreme of Fortune.) This made a great noise when it appeared. Charles V. of France had it transcribed for his library, and translated; and it was afterwards translated into Italian and Spanish.

Petrarch returned to Milan, and passed the autumn at his house, the Linterno, where he met with an accident, that for some time threatened dangerous consequences. He thus relates it, in a letter to his friend, Neri Morandi:—"I have a great volume of the epistles of Cicero, which I have taken the pains to transcribe myself, for the copyists understand nothing. One day, when I was entering my library, my gown got entangled with this large book, so that the volume fell heavily on my left leg, a little above the heel. By some fatality, I treated the accident too lightly. I walked, I rode on horseback, according to my usual custom; but my leg became inflamed, the skin changed colour, and mortification began to appear. The pain took away my cheerfulness and sleep. I then perceived that it was foolish courage to trifle with so serious an accident. Doctors were called in. They feared at first that it would be necessary to amputate the limb; but, at last, by means of regimen and fomentation, the afflicted member was put into the way of healing. It is singular that, ever since my infancy, my misfortunes have always fallen on this same left leg. In truth, I have always been tempted to believe in destiny; and why not, if, by the word destiny, we understand Providence?"

As soon as his leg was recovered, he made a trip to Bergamo. There was in that city a jeweller named Enrico Capri, a man of great natural talents, who cherished a passionate admiration for the learned, and above all for Petrarch, whose likeness was pictured or statued in every room of his house. He had copies made at a great expense of everything that came from his pen. He implored Petrarch to come and see him at Bergamo. "If he honours my household gods," he said, "but for a single day with his presence, I shall be happy all my life, and famous through all futurity." Petrarch consented, and on the 13th of October, 1358, the poet was received at Bergamo with transports of joy. The governor of the country and the chief men of the city wished to lodge him in some palace; but Petrarch adhered to his jeweller, and would not take any other lodging but with his friend.

A short time after his return to Milan, Petrarch had the pleasure of welcoming to his house John Boccaccio, who passed some days with him. The author of the Decamerone regarded Petrarch as his literary master. He owed him a still higher obligation, according to his own statement; namely, that of converting his heart, which, he says, had been frivolous and inclined to gallantry, and even to licentiousness, until he received our poet's advice. He was about forty-five years old when he went to Milan. Petrarch made him sensible that it was improper, at his age, to lose his time in courting women; that he ought to employ it more seriously, and turn towards heaven, the devotion which he misplaced on earthly beauties. This conversation is the subject of one of Boccaccio's eclogues, entitled, "Philostropos." His eclogues are in the style of Petrarch, obscure and enigmatical, and the subjects are muffled up under emblems and Greek names.

After spending some days with Petrarch, that appeared short to them both, Boccaccio, pressed by business, departed about the beginning of April, 1359. The great novelist soon afterwards sent to Petrarch from Florence a beautiful copy of Dante's poem, written in his own hand, together with some indifferent Latin verses, in which he bestows the highest praises on the author of the Inferno. At that time, half the world believed that Petrarch was jealous of Dante's fame; and the rumour was rendered plausible by the circumstance—for which he has accounted very rationally—that he had not a copy of Dante in his library.

In the month of May in this year, 1359, a courier from Bohemia brought Petrarch a letter from the Empress Anne, who had the condescension to write to him with her own hand to inform him that she had given birth to a daughter. Great was the joy on this occasion, for the Empress had been married five years, but, until now, had been childless. Petrarch, in his answer, dated the 23rd of the same month, after expressing his sense of the honour which her Imperial Majesty had done him, adds some common-places, and seasons them with his accustomed pedantry. He pronounces a grand eulogy on the numbers of the fair sex who had distinguished themselves by their virtues and their courage. Among these he instances Isis, Carmenta, the mother of Evander, Sappho, the Sybils, the Amazons, Semiramis, Tomiris, Cleopatra, Zenobia, the Countess Matilda, Lucretia, Cornelia, the mother of the Gracchi, Martia, Portia, and Livia. The Empress Anne was no doubt highly edified by this muster-roll of illustrious women; though some of the heroines, such as Lucretia, might have bridled up at their chaste names being classed with that of Cleopatra.

Petrarch repaired to Linterno, on the 1st of October, 1359; but his stay there was very short. The winter set in sooner than usual. The constant rains made his rural retreat disagreeable, and induced him to return to the city about the end of the month.

On rising, one morning, soon after his return to Milan, he found that he had been robbed of everything valuable in his house, excepting his books. As it was a domestic robbery, he could accuse nobody of it but his son John and his servants, the former of whom had returned from Avignon. On this, he determined to quit his house at St. Ambrosio, and to take a small lodging in the city; here, however, he could not live in peace. His son and servants quarrelled every day, in his very presence, so violently that they exchanged blows. Petrarch then lost all patience, and turned the whole of his pugnacious inmates out of doors. His son John had now become an arrant debauchee; and it was undoubtedly to supply his debaucheries that he pillaged his own father. He pleaded strongly to be readmitted to his home; but Petrarch persevered for some time in excluding him, though he ultimately took him back.

It appears from one of Petrarch's letters, that many people at Milan doubted his veracity about the story of the robbery, alleging that it was merely a pretext to excuse his inconstancy in quitting his house at St. Ambrosio; but that he was capable of accusing his own son on false grounds is a suspicion which the whole character of Petrarch easily repels. He went and settled himself in the monastery of St. Simplician, an abbey of the Benedictines of Monte Cassino, pleasantly situated without the walls of the city.

He was scarcely established in his new home at St. Simplician's, when Galeazzo Visconti arrived in triumph at Milan, after having taken possession of Pavia. The capture of this city much augmented the power of the Lords of Milan; and nothing was wanting to their satisfaction but the secure addition to their dominions of Bologna, to which Barnabo Visconti was laying siege, although John of Olegea had given it up to the Church in consideration of a pension and the possession of the city of Fermo.

This affair had thrown the court of Avignon into much embarrassment, and the Pope requested Nicholas Acciajuoli, Grand Seneschal of Naples, who had been sent to the Papal city by his Neapolitan Majesty, to return by way of Milan, and there negotiate a peace between the Church and Barnabo Visconti. Acciajuoli reached Milan at the end of May, very eager to see Petrarch, of whom he had heard much, without having yet made his acquaintance. Petrarch describes their first interview in a letter to Zanobi da Strada, and seems to have been captivated by the gracious manners of the Grand Seneschal.

With all his popularity, the Seneschal was not successful in his mission. When the Seneschal's proposals were read to the impetuous Barnabo, he said, at the end of every sentence "Io voglio Bologna." It is said that Petrarch detached Galeazzo Visconti from the ambitious projects of his brother; and that it was by our poet's advice that Galeazzo made a separate peace with the Pope; though, perhaps, the true cause of his accommodation with the Church was his being in treaty with France and soliciting the French monarch's daughter, Isabella, in marriage for his son Giovanni. After this marriage had been celebrated with magnificent festivities, Petrarch was requested by Galeazzo to go to Paris, and to congratulate the unfortunate King John upon his return to his country. Our poet had a transalpine prejudice against France;

but he undertook this mission to its capital, and was deeply touched by its unfortunate condition.

If the aspect of the country in general was miserable, that of the capital was still worse. "Where is Paris," exclaims Petrarch, "that metropolis, which, though inferior to its reputation, was, nevertheless, a great city?" He tells us that its streets were covered with briars and grass, and that it looked like a vast desert.

Here, however, in spite of its desolate condition, Petrarch witnessed the joy with which the Parisians received their King John and the Dauphin Charles. The King had not been well educated, yet he respected literature and learned men. The Dauphin was an accomplished prince; and our poet says that he was captivated by his modesty, sense, and information.

Petrarch arrived at Milan early in March, 1361, bringing letters from King John and his son the Dauphin, in which those princes entreat the two Lords of Milan to persuade Petrarch by every means to come and establish himself at their court. No sooner had he refused their pressing invitations, than he received an equally earnest request from the Emperor to accept his hospitality at Prague.

At this period, it had given great joy in Bohemia that the Empress had produced a son, and that the kingdom now possessed an heir apparent. His Imperial Majesty's satisfaction made him, for once, generous, and he distributed rich presents among his friends. Nor was our poet forgotten on this occasion. The Emperor sent him a gold embossed cup of admirable workmanship, accompanied by a letter, expressing his high regard, and repeating his request that he would pay him a visit in Germany. Petrarch returned him a letter of grateful thanks, saying: "Who would not be astonished at seeing transferred to my use a vase consecrated by the mouth of Cæsar? But I will not profane the sacred gift by the common use of it. It shall adorn my table only on days of solemn festivity." With regard to the Imperial invitation, he concludes a long apology for not accepting it immediately, but promising that, as soon as the summer was over, if he could find a companion for the journey, he would go to the court of Prague, and remain as long as it pleased his Majesty, since the presence of Cæsar would console him for the absence of his books, his friends, and his country. This epistle is dated July 17th, 1861.

Petrarch quitted Milan during this year, a removal for which various reasons are alleged by his biographers, though none of them appear to me quite satisfactory.

He had now a new subject of grief to descant upon. The Marquis of Montferrat, unable to contend against the Visconti, applied to the Pope for assistance. He had already made a treaty with the court of London, by which it was agreed that a body of English troops were to be sent to assist the Marquis against the Visconti. They entered Italy by Nice. It was the first time that our countrymen had ever entered the

Saturnian land. They did no credit to the English character for humanity, but ravaged lands and villages, killing men and violating women. Their general appellation was the bulldogs of England. What must have been Petrarch's horror at these unkennelled hounds! In one of his letters he vents his indignation at their atrocities; but, by-and-by, in the same epistle, he glides into his bookworm habit of apostrophizing the ancient heroes of Rome, Brutus, Camillus, and God knows how many more!

The plague now again broke out in Italy; and the English and other predatory troops contributed much to spread its ravages. It extended to many places; but most of all it afflicted Milan.

It is probable that these disasters were among the causes of Petrarch's leaving Milan. He settled at Padua, when the plague had not reached it. At this time, Petrarch lost his son John. Whether he died at Milan or at Padua is not certain, but, wherever he died, it was most probably of the plague. John had not quite attained his twenty-fourth year.

In the same year, 1361, he married his daughter Francesca, now near the age of twenty, to Francesco di Brossano, a gentleman of Milan. Petrarch speaks highly of his son-in-law's talents, and of the mildness of his character. Boccaccio has drawn his portrait in the most pleasing colours. Of the poet's daughter, also, he tells us, "that without being handsome, she had a very agreeable face, and much resembled her father." It does not seem that she inherited his genius; but she was an excellent wife, a tender mother, and a dutiful daughter. Petrarch was certainly pleased both with her and with his son-in-law; and, if he did not live with the married pair, he was, at least, near them, and much in their society.

When our poet arrived at Padua, Francesco di Carrara, the son of his friend Jacopo, reigned there in peace and alone. He had inherited his father's affection for Petrarch. Here, too, was his friend Pandolfo Malatesta, one of the bravest condottieri of the fourteenth century, who had been driven away from Milan by the rage and jealousy of Barnabo.

The plague, which still continued to infest Southern Europe in 1362, had even in the preceding year deprived our poet of his beloved friend Socrates, who died at Avignon. "He was," says Petrarch, "of all men the dearest to my heart. His sentiments towards me never varied during an acquaintance of thirty-one years."

The plague and war rendered Italy at this time so disagreeable to Petrarch, that he resolved on returning to Vaucluse. He, therefore, set out from Padua for Milan, on the 10th of January, 1362, reckoning that when the cold weather was over he might depart from the latter place on his route to Avignon. But when he reached Milan, he found that the state of the country would not permit him to proceed to the Alps.

The Emperor of Germany now sent Petrarch a third letter of invitation to come and see him, which our poet promised to accept; but alleged that he was prevented by the impossibility of getting a safe passage. Boccaccio, hearing that Petrarch meditated a journey to the far North, was much alarmed, and reproached him for his intention of dragging the Muses into Sarmatia, when Italy was the true Parnassus.

The Library of St. Mark, St. Mark's Place, Venice.

In June, 1362, the plague, which had begun its ravages at Padua, chased Petrarch from that place, and he took the resolution of establishing himself at Venice, which it had not reached. The course of the pestilence, like that of the cholera, was not general, but unaccountably capricious. Villani says that it acted like hail, which will desolate fields to the right and left, whilst it spares those in the middle. The war had not permitted our poet to travel either to Avignon or into Germany. The plague had driven him out of Milan and Padua. "I am not flying from death," he said, "but seeking repose."

Having resolved to repair to Venice, Petrarch as usual took his books along with him. From one of his letters to Boccaccio, it appears that it was his intention to bestow his library on some religious community, but, soon after his arrival at Venice, he conceived the idea of offering this treasure to the Venetian Republic. He wrote to the Government that he wished the blessed Evangelist, St. Mark, to be the heir of those books, on condition that they should all be placed in safety, that they should neither be sold nor separated, and that they should be sheltered from fire and water, and carefully preserved for the use and amusement of the learned and noble in Venice. He expressed his hopes, at the same time, that the illustrious city would acquire other trusts of the same kind for the good of the public, and that the citizens who loved their country, the nobles above all, and even strangers, would follow his example in bequeathing books to the church of St. Mark, which might one day contain a great collection similar to those of the ancients.

The procurators of the church of St. Mark having offered to defray the expense of lodging and preserving his library, the republic decreed that our poet's offer did honour to the Venetian state. They assigned to Petrarch for his own residence a large palace, called the Two Towers, formerly belonging to the family of Molina. The mansion was very lofty, and commanded a prospect of the harbour. Our poet took great pleasure in this view, and describes it with vivid interest. "From this port," he says, "I see vessels departing, which are as large as the house I inhabit, and which have masts taller than its towers. These ships resemble a mountain floating on the sea; they go to all parts of the world amidst a thousand dangers; they carry our wines to the English, our honey to the Scythians, our saffron, our oils, and our linen to the Syrians, Armenians, Persians, and Arabians; and, wonderful to say, convey our wood to the Greeks and Egyptians. From all these countries they bring back in return articles of merchandise, which they diffuse over all Europe. They go even as far as the Tanais. The navigation of our seas does not extend farther north; but, when they have arrived there, they quit their vessels, and travel on to trade with India and China; and, after passing the Caucasus and the Ganges, they proceed as far as the Eastern Ocean."

It is natural to suppose that Petrarch took all proper precautions for the presentation of his books; nevertheless, they are not now to be seen at Venice. Tomasini tells us that they had been placed at the top of the church of St. Mark, that he demanded a sight of them, but that he found them almost entirely spoiled, and some of them even petrified.

Whilst Petrarch was forming his new establishment at Venice, the news arrived that Pope Innocent VI. had died on the 12th of September. "He was a good, just, and simple man," says the continuator of Nangis. A simple man he certainly was, for he believed Petrarch to be a sorcerer on account of his reading Virgil. Innocent was succeeded in the pontificate, to the surprise of all the world, by William Grimoard, abbot of St. Victor at Marseilles, who took the title of Urban V. The Cardinals chose him, though he was not of their Sacred College, from their jealousy lest a pope should be elected from the opposite party of their own body. Petrarch rejoiced at his election, and ascribed it to the direct interference of Heaven. De Sade says that the new Pope desired Petrarch to be the apostolic secretary, but that he was not to be tempted by a gilded chain.

About this time Petrarch received news of the death of Azzo Correggio, one of his dearest friends, whose widow and children wrote to him on this occasion, the latter telling him that they regarded him as a father.

Boccaccio came to Venice to see Petrarch in 1363, and their meeting was joyous. They spent delightfully together the months of June, July, and August, 1363. Boccaccio had not long left him, when, in the following year, our poet heard of the death of his friend Lælius, and his tears were still fresh for his loss, when he received another shock in being bereft of Simonides. It requires a certain age and degree of experience to appreciate this kind of calamity, when we feel the desolation of losing our accustomed friends, and almost wish ourselves out of life that we may escape from its solitude. Boccaccio returned to Florence early in September, 1363.

In 1364, peace was concluded between Barnabo Visconti and Urban V. Barnabo having refused to treat with the Cardinal Albornoz, whom he personally hated, his Holiness sent the Cardinal Androine de la Roche to Italy as his legate. Petrarch repaired to Bologna to pay his respects to the new representative of the Pope. He was touched by the sad condition in which he found that city, which had been so nourishing when he studied at its university. "I seem," he says, "to be in a dream when I see the once fair city desolated by war, by slavery, and by famine. Instead of the joy that once reigned here, sadness is everywhere spread, and you hear only sighs and wailings in place of songs. Where you formerly saw troops of girls dancing, there are now only bands of robbers and assassins."

Lucchino del Verme, one of the most famous condottieri of his time, had commanded troops in the service of the Visconti, at whose court he made the acquaintance of Petrarch. Our poet invited him to serve the Venetians in the war in which they were engaged with the people of Candia. Lucchino went to Venice whilst Petrarch was absent, reviewed the troops, and embarked for Candia on board the fleet, which consisted of thirty galleys and eight large vessels. Petrarch did not return to Venice till the expedition had sailed. He passed the summer in the country, having at his house one of his friends, Barthelemi di Pappazuori, Bishop of Christi, whom he had known at Avignon, and who had come purposely to see him. One day, when they were both at a window which overlooked the sea, they beheld one of the long vessels which the Italians call a galeazza, entering the harbour. The green branches with which it was decked, the air of joy that appeared among the mariners, the young men crowned with laurel, who, from the prow, saluted the standard of their country—everything betokened that the galeazza brought good news. When the vessel came a little nearer, they could perceive the captured colours of their enemies suspended from the poop, and no doubt could be entertained that a great victory had been won.

The moment that the sentinel on the tower had made the signal of a vessel entering the harbour, the people flocked thither in crowds, and their joy was even beyond expectation when they learned that the rebellion had been totally crushed, and the island reduced to obedience. The most magnificent festivals were given at Venice on this occasion.

Shortly after these Venetian fêtes, we find our poet writing a long letter to Boccaccio, in which he gives a curious and interesting description of the Jongleurs of Italy. He speaks of them in a very different manner from those pictures that have come down to us of the Provençal Troubadours. The latter were at once poets and musicians, who frequented the courts and castles of great lords, and sang their praises. Their strains, too, were sometimes satirical. They amused themselves with different subjects, and wedded their verses to the sound of the harp and other instruments. They were called Troubadours from the word *trobar*, "to invent." They were original poets, of the true minstrel breed, similar to those whom Bishop Percy ascribes to England in the olden time, but about the reality of whom, as a professional body, Ritson has shown some cause to doubt. Of the Italian Jongleurs, Petrarch gives us a humble notion. "They are a class," he says, "who have little wit, but a great deal of memory, and still more impudence. Having nothing of their own to recite, they snatch at what they can get from others, and go about to the courts of princes to declaim verses, in the vulgar tongue, which they have got by heart. At those courts they insinuate themselves into the favour of the great, and get subsistence and presents. They seek their means of livelihood, that is, the verses they recite, among the best authors, from whom they obtain, by dint of solicitation, and even by bribes of money, compositions for their rehearsal. I have often repelled their importunities, but sometimes, touched by their entreaties, I have spent hours in composing productions for them. I have seen them leave me in rags and poverty, and return, some time afterwards, clothed in silks, and with purses well furnished, to thank me for having relieved them."

In the course of the same amusing correspondence with Boccaccio, which our poet maintained at this period, he gives an account of an atheist and blasphemer at Venice, with whom he had a long conversation. It ended in our poet seizing the infidel by the mantle, and ejecting him from his house with unceremonious celerity. This conclusion of their dialogue gives us a higher notion of Petrarch's piety than of his powers of argument.

Petrarch went to spend the autumn of 1365 at Pavia, which city Galeazzo Visconti made his principal abode. To pass the winter till Easter, our poet returned first to Venice, and then to Padua, according to his custom, to do the duties of his canonry. It was then that his native Florence, wishing to recall a man who did her so much honour, thought of asking for him from the Pope the canonry of either Florence or Fiesole. Petrarch fully appreciated the shabby kindness of his countrymen. A republic that could afford to be lavish in all other expenses, limited their bounty towards him to the begging of a canonicate for him from his Holiness, though Florence had confiscated his father's property. But the Pope had other views for him, and had actually appointed him to the canonry of Carpentras, when a false rumour of his death unhappily induced the Pontiff to dispose not only of that living, but of Parma and others which he had resigned to indigent friends.

During the February of 1366 there was great joy in the house of Petrarch, for his daughter, Francesca, the wife of Francesco di Brossano, gave birth to a boy, whom Donato degli Albanzani, a peculiarly-favoured friend of the poet's, held over the baptismal font, whilst he was christened by the name of Francesco.

Meanwhile, our poet was delighted to hear of reformations in the Church, which signalized the commencement of Urban V.'s pontificate. After some hesitation, Petrarch ventured to write a strong advice to the Pope to remove the holy seat from Avignon to Rome. His letter is long, zealous, superstitious, and, as usual, a little pedantic. The Pope did not need this epistle to spur his intentions as to replacing the holy seat at Rome; but it so happened that he did make the removal no very long time after Petrarch had written to him.

On the 20th of July, 1366, our poet rose, as was his custom, to his matin devotions, and reflected that he was precisely then entering on his sixty-third year. He wrote to Boccaccio on the subject. He repeats the belief, at that time generally entertained, that the sixty-third year of a man's life is its most dangerous crisis. It was a belief connected with astrology, and a superstitious idea of the influence of numbers; of course, if it retains any attention at present, it must subsist on practical observation: and I have heard sensible physicians, who had no faith in the influence of the stars, confess that they thought that time of life, commonly called the grand climacteric, a critical period for the human constitution.

In May, 1367, Pope Urban accomplished his determination to remove his court from Avignon in spite of the obstinacy of his Cardinals; but he did not arrive at Rome till the month of October. He was joyously received by the Romans; and, in addition to other compliments, had a long letter from Petrarch, who was then at Venice. Some days after the date of this letter, our poet received one from Galeazzo Visconti. The Pope, it seems, wished, at whatever price, to exterminate the Visconti. He thundered this year against Barnabo with a terrible bull, in which he published a crusade against him. Barnabo, to whom, with all his faults, the praise of courage cannot be denied, brought down his troops from the Po, in order to ravage Mantua, and to make himself master of that city. Galeazzo, his brother, less warlike, thought of employing negotiation for appeasing the storm; and he invited Petrarch to Pavia, whither our poet arrived in 1368. He attempted to procure a peace for the Visconti, but was not successful.

It was not, however, solely to treat for a peace with his enemies that Galeazzo drew our poet to his court. He was glad that he should be present at the marriage of his daughter Violante with Lionel, Duke of Clarence, son of Edward III. of England. The young English prince, followed by many nobles of our land, passed through France, and arrived at Milan on the 14th of May. His nuptials took place about a month later. At the marriage-dinner Petrarch was seated at the table where there were only princes, or nobles of the first rank. It is a curious circumstance that Froissart, so well known as an historian of England, came at this time to Milan, in the suite of the Duke of Clarence, and yet formed no acquaintance with our poet. Froissart was then only about thirty years old. It might have been hoped that the two geniuses would have become intimate friends; but there is no trace of their having even spoken to each other. Petrarch's neglect of Froissart may not have been so wonderful; but it is strange that the latter should not have been ambitious to pay his court to the greatest poet then alive. It is imaginable, however, that Petrarch, with all his natural gentleness, was proud in his demeanour to strangers; and if so, Froissart was excusable for an equally-proud reserve.

In the midst of the fêtes that were given for the nuptials of the English prince, Petrarch received news of the death of his grandchild. This little boy had died at Pavia, on the very day of the marriage of Lionel and Violante, when only two years and four months old. Petrarch caused a marble mausoleum to be erected over him, and twelve Latin lines of his own composition to be engraved upon it. He was deeply touched by the loss of his little grandson. "This child," he says, "had a singular resemblance to me, insomuch that any one who had not seen its mother would have taken me for its father."

A most interesting letter from Boccaccio to our poet found Petrarch at Pavia, whither he had retired from Milan, wearied with the marriage fêtes. The summer season was now approaching, when he was accustomed to be ill; and he had, besides, got by the accident of a fall a bad contusion on his leg. He was anxious to return to Padua, and wished to embark on the Po. But war was abroad; the river banks were crowded with troops of the belligerent parties; and no boatmen could be found for some time who would go with him for love or money. At last, he found the master of a vessel bold enough to take him aboard. Any other vessel would have been attacked and pillaged; but Petrarch had no fear; and, indeed, he was stopped in his river passage only to be loaded with presents. He arrived in safety at Padua, on the 9th of June, 1368.

The Pope wished much to see our poet at Rome; but Petrarch excused himself on account of his health and the summer season, which was always trying to him. But he promised to repair to his Holiness as soon as his health should permit, not to ask benefices of the holy father, but only his blessing. During the same year, we find Petrarch complaining often and painfully of his bodily infirmities. In a letter to Coluccio Salutati, he says:—"Age, which makes others garrulous, only makes me silent. When young, I used to write many and long letters. At present, I write only to my particular friends, and even to them very short letters." Petrarch was now sixty-four years old. He had never seen Pope Urban V., as he tells us himself; but he was very desirous of seeing him, and of seeing Rome adorned by the two great luminaries of the world, the Pope and the Emperor. Pope Urban, fearing the heats of Italy, to which he was not accustomed, had gone to pass the dog-days at Monte-Fiascone. When he returned to Rome, in October, on his arrival at the Colline gate, near the church of St. Angelo, he found the Emperor, who was waiting for him. The Emperor, the moment he saw his Holiness, dismounted from his horse, took the reins of that of the Pope, and conducted him on foot to the church of St. Peter. As to this submission of civil to ecclesiastical dignity, different opinions were entertained, even at Rome; and the wiser class of men disapproved of it. Petrarch's opinion on the subject is not recorded; but, during this year, there is no proof that he had any connection with the Emperor; and my own opinion is that he did not approve of his conduct. It is certain that Petrarch condemned the Pope's entering Rome at the head of 2000 soldiery. "The Roman Pontiff," he remarks, "should trust to his dignity and to his sanctity, when coming into our capital, and not to an army with their swords and cuirasses. The cross of Jesus is the only standard which he ought to rear. Trumpets and drums were out of place. It would have been enough to have sung hallelujahs."

Petrarch, in his letter to Boccaccio, in the month of September, says that he had got the fever; and he was still so feeble that he was obliged to employ the hand of a stranger in writing to him. He indites as follows:—"I have had the fever for forty days. It weakened me so much that I could not go to my church, though it is near my house, without being carried. I feel as if my health would never be restored. My constitution seems to be entirely worn out." In another letter to the Cardinal Cabassole, who informed him of the Pope's wish to see him, he says: "His Holiness does me more honour than I deserve. It is to you that I owe this obligation. Return a thousand thanks to the holy father in your own name and in mine." The Pope was so anxious to see Petrarch that he wrote to him with his own hand, reproaching him for refusing his invitation. Our poet, after returning a second apology, passed the winter in making preparations for this journey; but before setting out he thought proper to make his will. It was written with his own hand at Padua.

In his testament he forbids weeping for his death, justly remarking that tears do no good to the dead, and may do harm to the living. He asks only prayers and alms to the poor who will pray for him. "As for my burial," he says, "let it be made as my friends think fit. What signifies it to me where my body is laid?" He then makes some bequests in favour of the religious orders; and he founds an anniversary in his own church of Padua, which is still celebrated every year on the 9th of July.

Then come his legacies to his friends. He bequeathes to the Lord of Padua his picture of the Virgin, painted by Giotto; "the beauty of which," he says, "is little known to the ignorant, though the masters of art will never look upon it without admiration."

To Donato di Prato Vecchio, master of grammar at Venice, he leaves all the money that he had lent him. He bequeathes the horses he may have at his death to Bonzanello di Vigoncia and Lombardo da Serigo, two friends of his, citizens of Padua, wishing them to draw lots for the choice of the horses. He avows being indebted to Lombardo da Serigo 134 golden ducats, advanced for the expenses of his house. He also bequeathes to the same person a goblet of silver gilt (undoubtedly the same which the Emperor Charles had sent him in 1362). He leaves to John Abucheta, warden of his church, his great breviary, which he bought at Venice for 100 francs, on condition that, after his death, this breviary shall remain in the sacristy for the use of the future priests of the church. To John Boccaccio he bequeathes 50 gold florins of Florence, to buy him a winter-habit for his studies at night. "I am ashamed," he adds, "to leave so small a sum to so great a man;" but he entreats his friends in general to impute the smallness of their legacies to that of his fortune. To Tomaso Bambasi, of Ferrara, he makes a present of his good lute, that he may make use of it in singing the praises of God. To Giovanni Dandi, physician of Padua, he leaves 50 ducats of gold, to buy a gold ring, which he may wear in remembrance of him.

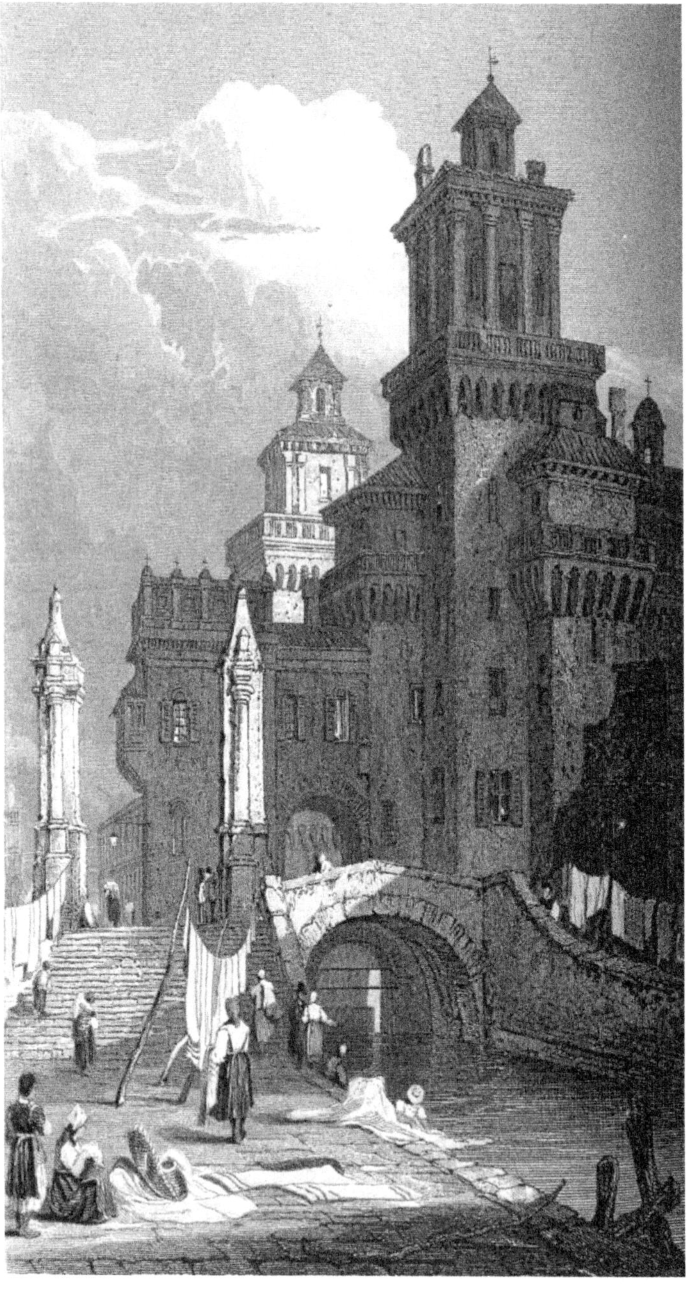

Ferrara.

He appoints Francesco da Brossano, citizen of Milan, his heir, and desires him, not only as his heir, but as his dear son, to divide into two parts the money he should find —the one for himself, the other for the person to whom it was assigned. "It would seem by this," says De Sade, "that Petrarch would not mention his daughter by name in a public will, because she was not born in marriage." Yet his shyness to name her makes it singular that he should style Brossano his son. In case Brossano should die before him, he appoints Lombardo da Serigo his eventual heir. De Sade considers the appointment as a deed of trust. With respect to his little property at Vaucluse, he leaves it to the hospital in that diocese. His last bequest is to his brother Gherardo, a Carthusian of Montrieux. He desires his heir to write to him immediately after his decease, and to give him the option of a hundred florins of gold, payable at once, or by five or ten florins every year.

A few days after he had made this will, he set out for Rome. The pleasure with which he undertook the journey made him suppose that he could support it. But when he reached Ferrara he fell down in a fit, in which he continued thirty hours, without sense or motion; and it was supposed that he was dead. The most violent remedies were used to restore him to consciousness, but he says that he felt them no more than a statue.

Nicholas d'Este II., the son of Obizzo, was at that time Lord of Ferrara, a friend and admirer of Petrarch. The physicians thought him dead, and the whole city was in grief. The news spread to Padua, Venice, Milan, and Pavia. Crowds came from all parts to his burial. Ugo d'Este, the brother of Nicholas, a young man of much merit, who had an enthusiastic regard for Petrarch, paid him unremitting attention during his illness. He came three or four times a day to see him, and sent messengers incessantly to inquire how he was. Our poet acknowledged that he owed his life to the kindness of those two noblemen.

When Petrarch was recovering, he was impatient to pursue his route, though the physicians assured him that he could not get to Rome alive. He would have attempted the journey in spite of their warnings, if his strength had seconded his desires, but he was unable to sit his horse. They brought him back to Padua, laid on a soft seat on a boat. His unhoped-for return caused as much surprise as joy in that city, where he was received by its lords and citizens with as much joy as if he had come back from the other world. To re-establish his health, he went to a village called Arquà, situated on the slope of a hill famous for the salubrity of its air, the goodness of its wines, and the beauty of its vineyards. An everlasting spring reigns there, and the place commands a view of pleasingly-scattered villas. Petrarch built himself a house on the high ground of the village, and he added to the vines of the country a great number of other fruit-trees.

Petrarch's house at Arquà.

He had scarcely fixed himself at Arquà, when he put his last hand to a work which he had begun in the year 1367. To explain the subject of this work, and the circumstances which gave rise to it, I think it necessary to state what was the real cause of our poet's disgust at Venice. He appeared there, no doubt, to lead an agreeable life among many friends, whose society was delightful to him. But there reigned in this city what Petrarch thought licentiousness in conversation. The most ignorant persons were in the habit of undervaluing the finest geniuses. It fills one with regret to find Petrarch impatient of a liberty of speech, which, whatever its abuses may be, cannot be suppressed, without crushing the liberty of human thought. At Venice, moreover, the philosophy of Aristotle was much in vogue, if doctrines could be called Aristotelian, which had been disfigured by commentators, and still worse garbled by Averroes. The disciples of Averroes at Venice insisted on the world having been co-eternal with God, and made a joke of Moses and his book of Genesis. "Would the eternal architect," they said, "remain from all eternity doing nothing? Certainly not! The world's youthful appearance is owing to its revolutions, and the changes it has undergone by deluges and conflagrations." "Those free-thinkers," Petrarch tells us, "had a great contempt for Christ and his Apostles, as well as for all those who did not bow the knee to the Stagirite." They called the doctrines of Christianity fables, and hell and heaven the tales of asses. Finally, they believed that Providence takes no care of anything under the region of the moon. Four young Venetians of this sect had attached themselves to Petrarch, who endured their society, but opposed their opinions. His opposition offended them, and they resolved to humble him in the public estimation. They constituted themselves a tribunal to try his merits: they appointed an advocate to plead for him, and they concluded by determining that he was a good man, but illiterate!

This affair made a great stir at Venice. Petrarch seems at first to have smiled with sensible contempt at so impertinent a farce; but will it be believed that his friends, and among them Donato and Boccaccio, advised and persuaded him to treat it seriously, and to write a book about it? Petrarch accordingly put his pen to the subject. He wrote a treatise, which he entitled "De sui ipsius et aliorum Ignorantia—" (On his own Ignorance, and on that of others).

Petrarch had himself formed the design of confuting the doctrines of Averroes; but he engaged Ludovico Marsili, an Augustine monk of Florence, to perform the task. This monk, in Petrarch's opinion, possessed great natural powers, and our poet exhorts him to write against that rabid animal (Averroes) who barks with so much fury against Christ and his Apostles. Unfortunately, the rabid animals who write against the truths we are most willing to believe are difficult to be killed.

The good air of the Euganean mountains failed to re-establish the health of

Petrarch. He continued ill during the summer of 1370. John di Dondi, his physician, or rather his friend, for he would have no physician, would not quit Padua without going to see him. He wrote to him afterwards that he had discovered the true cause of his disease, and that it arose from his eating fruits, drinking water, and frequent fastings. His medical adviser, also, besought him to abstain from all salted meats, and raw fruits, or herbs. Petrarch easily renounced salted provisions, "but, as to fruits," he says, "Nature must have been a very unnatural mother to give us such agreeable food, with such delightful hues and fragrance, only to seduce her children with poison covered over with honey."

Avignon.

Whilst Petrarch was thus ill, he received news very unlikely to forward his recovery. The Pope took a sudden resolution to return to Avignon. That city, in concert with the Queen of Naples and the Kings of France and Arragon, sent him vessels to convey him to Avignon. Urban gave as a reason for his conduct the necessity of making peace between the crowns of France and England, but no one doubted that the love of his own country, the difficulty of inuring himself to the climate of Rome, the enmity and rebellious character of the Italians, and the importunities of his Cardinals, were the true cause of his return. He was received with great demonstrations of joy; but St. Bridget had told him that if he went to Avignon he should die soon afterwards, and it so happened that her prophecy was fulfilled, for the Pope not long after his arrival in Provence was seized with a mortal illness, and died on the 19th of December, 1370. In the course of his pontificate, he had received two singular honours. The Emperor of the West had performed the office of his equerry, and the Emperor of the East abjured schism, acknowledging him as primate of the whole Christian Church.

The Cardinals chose as Urban's successor a man who did honour to their election, namely, Pietro Rogero, nephew of Clement VI., who took the name of Gregory XI. Petrarch knew him, he had seen him at Padua in 1307, when the Cardinal was on his way to Rome, and rejoiced at his accession. The new Pontiff caused a letter to be written to our poet, expressing his wish to see him, and to be of service to him.

In a letter written about this time to his friend Francesco Bruni, we perceive that Petrarch is not quite so indifferent to the good things of the world as the general tenor of his letters would lead us to imagine. He writes:—"Were I to say that I want means to lead the life of a canon, I should be wrong, but when I say that my single self have more acquaintances than all the chapter put together, and, consequently, that I am put to more expenses in the way of hospitality, then I am right. This embarrassment increases every day, and my resources diminish. I have made vain efforts to free myself from my difficulties. My prebend, it is true, yields me more bread and wine than I need for my own consumption. I can even sell some of it. But my expenses are very considerable. I have never less than two horses, usually five or six amanuenses. I have only three at this moment. It is because I could find no more. Here it is easier to find a painter than an amanuensis. I have a venerable priest, who never quits me when I am at church. Sometimes when I count upon dining with him alone, behold, a crowd of guests will come in. I must give them something to eat, and I must tell them amusing stories, or else pass for being proud or avaricious.

"I am desirous to found a little oratory for the Virgin Mary; and shall do so, though I should sell or pawn my books. After that I shall go to Avignon, if my strength permits. If it does not, I shall send one of my people to the Cardinal Cabassole, and to you, that you may attempt to accomplish what I have often wished, but uselessly, as both you and he well know. If the holy father wishes to stay my old age, and put me into somewhat better circumstances, as he appears to me to wish, and as his predecessor promised me, the thing would be very easy. Let him do as it may please him, much, little, or nothing; I shall be always content. Only let him not say to me as Clement VI. used to do, 'ask what you wish for.' I cannot do so, for several reasons. In the first place, I do not myself know exactly what would suit me. Secondly, if I were to demand some vacant place, it might be given away before my demand reached the feet of his Holiness. Thirdly, I might make a request that might displease him. His extreme kindness might pledge him to grant it; and I should be made miserable by obtaining it.

"Let him give me, then, whatever he pleases, without waiting for my petitioning for it. Would it become me, at my years, to be a solicitor for benefices, having never been so in my youth? I trust, in this matter, to what you may do with the Cardinal Sabina. You are the only friends who remain to me in that country. These thirty years the Cardinal has given me marks of his affection and good-will. I am about to write to him a few words on the subject; and I shall refer him to this letter, to save my repeating to him those miserable little details with which I should not detain you, unless it seemed to be necessary."

A short time afterwards, Petrarch heard, with no small satisfaction, of the conduct of Cardinal Cabassole, at Perugia. When the Cardinal came to take leave of the Pope the evening before his departure for that city, he said, "Holy father, permit me to recommend Petrarch to you, on account of my love for him. He is, indeed, a man unique upon earth—a true phœnix." Scarcely was he gone, when the Cardinal of Boulogne, making pleasantries on the word phœnix, turned into ridicule both the praises of Cabassole and him who were their object. Francesco Bruni, in writing to Petrarch about the kindness of the one Cardinal, thought it unnecessary to report the pleasantries of the other. But Petrarch, who had heard of them from another quarter, relates them himself to Bruni, and says:—"I am not astonished. This man loved me formerly, and I was equally attached to him. At present he hates me, and I return his hatred. Would you know the reason of this double change? It is because he is the enemy of truth, and I am the enemy of falsehood; he dreads the liberty which inspires me, and I detest the pride with which he is swollen. If our fortunes were equal, and if we were together in a free place, I should not call myself a phœnix; for that title ill becomes me; but he would be an owl. Such people as he imagine, on account of riches ill-acquired, and worse employed, that they are at liberty to say what they please."

In the letter which Bruni wrote to Petrarch, to apprize him of Cabassole's departure, and of what he had said to the Pope in his favour, he gave him notice of the promotion of twelve new cardinals, whom Gregory had just installed, with a view to balance the domineering authority of the others. "And I fear," he adds, "that the Pope's obligations to satiate those new and hungry comers may retard the effects of his good-will towards you." "Let his Holiness satiate them," replied Petrarch; "let him appease their thirst, which is more than the Tagus, the Pactolus, and the ocean itself could do—I agree to it; and let him not think of me. I am neither famished nor thirsty. I shall content myself with their leavings, and with what the holy father may think meet to give, if he deigns to think of me."

Bruni was right. The Pope, beset by applications on all hands, had no time to think of Petrarch. Bruni for a year discontinued his correspondence. His silence vexed our poet. He wrote to Francesco, saying, "You do not write to me, because you cannot communicate what you would wish. You understand me ill, and you do me injustice. I desire nothing, and I hope for nothing, but an easy death. Nothing is more ridiculous than an old man's avarice; though nothing is more common. It is like a voyager wishing to heap up provisions for his voyage when he sees himself approaching the end of it. The holy father has written me a most obliging letter: is not that sufficient for me? I have not a doubt of his good-will towards me, but he is encompassed by people who thwart his intentions. Would that those persons could know how much I despise them, and how much I prefer my mediocrity to the vain grandeur which renders them so proud!" After a tirade against his enemies in purple, evidently some of the Cardinals, he reproaches Bruni for having dwelt so long for lucre in the ill-smelling Avignon; he exhorts him to leave it, and to come and end his days at Florence. He says that he does not write to the Pope for fear of appearing to remind him of his promises. "I have received," he adds, "his letter and Apostolic blessing; I beg you to communicate to his Holiness, in the clearest manner, that I wish for no more."

From this period Petrarch's health was never re-established. He was languishing with wishes to repair to Perugia, and to see his dear friend the Cardinal Cabassole. At the commencement of spring he mounted a horse, in order to see if he could support the journey; but his weakness was such that he could only ride a few steps. He wrote to the Cardinal expressing his regrets, but seems to console himself by recalling to his old friend the days they had spent together at Vaucluse, and their long walks, in which they often strayed so far, that the servant who came to seek for them and to announce that dinner was ready could not find them till the evening.

It appears from this epistle that our poet had a general dislike to cardinals. "You are not," he tells Cabassole, "like most of your brethren, whose heads are turned by a bit of red cloth so far as to forget that they are mortal men. It seems, on the contrary, as if honours rendered you more humble, and I do not believe that you would change your mode of thinking if they were to put a crown on your head." The good Cardinal, whom Petrarch paints in such pleasing colours, could not accustom himself to the climate of Italy. He had scarcely arrived there when he fell ill, and died on the 26th of August in the same year.

Of all the friends whom Petrarch had had at Avignon, he had now none left but Mattheus le Long, Archdeacon of Liege, with whom his ties of friendship had subsisted ever since they had studied together at Bologna. From him he received a letter on the 5th of January, 1372, and in his answer, dated the same day at Padua, he gives this picture of his condition, and of the life which he led:—

"You ask about my condition—it is this. I am, thanks to God, sufficiently tranquil, and free, unless I deceive myself, from all the passions of my youth. I enjoyed good health for a long time, but for two years past I have become infirm. Frequently, those around me have believed me dead, but I live still, and pretty much the same as you have known me. I could have mounted higher; but I wished not to do so, since every elevation is suspicious. I have acquired many friends and a good many books: I have lost my health and many friends; I have spent some time at Venice. At present I am at Padua, where I perform the functions of canon. I esteem myself happy to have quitted Venice, on account of that war which has been declared between that Republic and the Lord of Padua. At Venice I should have been suspected: here I am caressed. I pass the greater part of the year in the country, which I always prefer to the town. I repose, I write, I think; so you see that my way of life and my pleasures are the same as in my youth. Having studied so long it is astonishing that I have learnt so little. I hate nobody, I envy nobody. In that first season of life which is full of error and presumption, I despised all the world except myself. In middle life, I despised only myself. In my aged years, I despise all the world, and myself most of all. I fear only those whom I love. I desire only a good end. I dread a company of valets like a troop of robbers. I should have none at all, if my age and weakness permitted me. I am fain to shut myself up in concealment, for I cannot endure visits; it is an honour which displeases and wears me out. Amidst the Euganean hills I have built a small but neat mansion, where I reckon on passing quietly the rest of my days, having always before my eyes my dead or absent friends. To conceal nothing from you, I have been sought after by the Pope, the Emperor, and the King of France, who have given me pressing invitations, but I have constantly declined them, preferring my liberty to everything."

In this letter, Petrarch speaks of a sharp war that had arisen between Venice and Padua. A Gascon, named Rainier, who commanded the troops of Venice, having thrown bridges over the Brenta, established his camp at Abano, whence he sent detachments to ravage the lands of Padua. Petrarch was in great alarm; for Arquà is only two leagues from Abano. He set out on the 15th of November for Padua, to put himself and his books under protection. A friend at Verona wrote to him, saying, "Only write your name over the door of your house, and fear nothing; it will be your safeguard." The advice, it is hardly necessary to say, was absurd. Among the pillaging soldiery there were thousands who could not have read the poet's name if they had seen it written, and of those who were accomplished enough to read, probably many who would have thought Petrarch as fit to be plundered as another man. Petrarch, therefore, sensibly replied, "I should be sorry to trust them. Mars respects not the favourites of the Muses; I have no such idea of my name, as that it would shelter me from the furies of war." He was even in pain about his domestics, whom he left at Arquà, and who joined him some days afterwards.

Pandolfo Malatesta, learning what was passing in the Paduan territory, and the danger to which Petrarch was exposed, sent to offer him his horses, and an escort to conduct him to Pesaro, which was at that time his residence. He was Lord of Pesaro and Fossombrone. The envoy of Pandolfo found our poet at Padua, and used every argument to second his Lord's invitation; but Petrarch excused himself on account of the state of his health, the insecurity of the highways, and the severity of the weather. Besides, he said that it would be disgraceful to him to leave Padua in the present circumstances, and that it would expose him to the suspicion of cowardice, which he never deserved.

Pandolfo earnestly solicited from Petrarch a copy of his Italian works. Our poet in answer says to him, "I have sent to you by your messenger these trifles which were the amusement of my youth. They have need of all your indulgence. It is shameful for an old man to send you things of this nature; but you have earnestly asked for them, and can I refuse you anything? With what grace could I deny you verses which are current in the streets, and are in the mouth of all the world, who prefer them to the more solid compositions that I have produced in my riper years?" This letter is dated at Padua, on the 4th of January, 1373. Pandolfo Malatesta died a short time after receiving it.

Several Powers interfered to mediate peace between Venice and Padua, but their negotiations ended in nothing, the spirits of both belligerents were so embittered. The Pope had sent as his nuncio for this purpose a young professor of law, named Uguzzone da Thiene, who was acquainted with Petrarch. He lodged with our poet when he came to Padua, and he communicated to him some critical remarks which had been written at Avignon on Petrarch's letter to Pope Urban V., congratulating him on his return to Rome. A French monk of the order of St. Bernard passed for the author of this work. As it spoke irreverently of Italy, it stirred up the bile of Petrarch, and made him resume the pen with his sickly hand. His answer to the offensive production flows with anger, and is harsh even to abusiveness. He declaims, as usual, in favour of Italy, which he adored, and against France, which he disliked.

After a suspension the war was again conducted with fury, till at last a peace was signed at Venice on the 11th of September, 1373. The conditions were hard and humiliating to the chief of Padua. The third article ordained that he should come in person, or send his son, to ask pardon of the Venetian Republic for the insults he had offered her, and swear inviolable fidelity to her. The Carrara sent his son Francesco Novello, and requested Petrarch to accompany him. Our poet had no great wish to do so, and had too good an excuse in the state of his health, which was still very fluctuating, but the Prince importuned him, and he thought that he could not refuse a favour to such a friend.

Francesco Novello, accompanied by Petrarch, and by a great suite of Paduan gentlemen, arrived at Venice on the 27th of September, where they were well received, especially the poet. On the following day the chiefs of the maiden city gave him a public audience. But, whether the majesty of the Venetian Senate affected Petrarch, or his illness returned by accident, so it was that he could not deliver the speech which he had prepared, for his memory failed him. But the universal desire to hear him induced the Senators to postpone their sitting to the following day. He then spoke with energy, and was extremely applauded. Francesco Novello begged pardon, and took the oath of fidelity.

Francesco da Carrara loved and revered Petrarch, and used to go frequently to see him without ceremony in his small mansion at Arquà. The Prince one day complained to him that he had written for all the world excepting himself. Petrarch thought long and seriously about what he should compose that might please the Carrara; but the task was embarrassing. To praise him directly might seem sycophantish and fulsome to the Prince himself. To censure him would be still more indelicate. To escape the difficulty, he projected a treatise on the best mode of governing a State, and on the qualities required in the person who has such a charge. This subject furnished occasion for giving indirect praises, and, at the same time, for pointing out some defects which he had remarked in his patron's government.

It cannot be denied that there are some excellent maxims respecting government in this treatise, and that it was a laudable work for the fourteenth century. But since that period the subject has been so often discussed by minds of the first order, that we should look in vain into Petrarch's Essay for any truths that have escaped their observation. Nature offers herself in virgin beauty to the primitive poet. But abstract truth comes not to the philosopher, till she has been tried by the test of time.

After his return from Venice, Petrarch only languished. A low fever, that undermined his constitution, left him but short intervals of health, but made no change in his mode of life; he passed the greater part of the day in reading or writing. It does not appear, however, that he composed any work in the course of the year 1374. A few letters to Boccaccio are all that can be traced to his pen during that period. Their date is not marked in them, but they were certainly written shortly before his death. None of them possess any particular interest, excepting that always in which he mentions the Decameron.

It seems at first sight not a little astonishing that Petrarch, who had been on terms of the strictest friendship with Boccaccio for twenty-four years, should never till now have read his best work. Why did not Boccaccio send him his Decameron long before? The solution of this question must be made by ascribing the circumstance to the author's sensitive respect for the austerely moral character of our poet.

It is not known by what accident the Decameron fell into Petrarch's hands, during the heat of the war between Venice and Padua. Even then his occupations did not permit him to peruse it thoroughly; he only slightly ran through it, after which he says in his letter to Boccaccio, "I have not read your book with sufficient attention to pronounce an opinion upon it; but it has given me great pleasure. That which is too free in the work is sufficiently excusable for the age at which you wrote it, for its elegant language, for the levity of the subject, for the class of readers to whom it is suited. Besides, in the midst of much gay and playful matter, several grave and pious thoughts are to be found. Like the rest of the world, I have been particularly struck by the beginning and the end. The description which you give of the state of our country during the plague, appeared to me most true and most pathetic. The story which forms the conclusion made so vivid an impression on me, that I wished to get it by heart, in order to repeat it to some of my friends."

Petrarch, perceiving that this touching story of Griseldis made an impression on all the world, had an idea of translating it into Latin, for those who knew not the vulgar tongue. The following anecdote respecting it is told by Petrarch himself: —"One of his friends, a man of knowledge and intellect, undertook to read it to a company; but he had hardly got into the midst of it, when his tears would not permit him to continue. Again he tried to resume the reading, but with no better success."

Another friend from Verona having heard what had befallen the Paduan, wished to try the same experiment; he took up the composition, and read it aloud from beginning to end without the smallest change of voice or countenance, and said, in returning the book, "It must be owned that this is a touching story, and I should have wept, also, if I believed it to be true; but it is clearly a fable. There never was and there never will be such a woman as Griseldis."[14]

This letter, which Petrarch sent to Boccaccio, accompanied by a Latin translation of his story, is dated, in a MS. of the French King's library, the 8th of June, 1374. It is perhaps, the last letter which he ever wrote. He complains in it of "mischievous people, who opened packets to read the letters contained in them, and copied what they pleased. Proceeding in their licence, they even spared themselves the trouble of transcription, and kept the packets themselves." Petrarch, indignant at those violators of the rights and confidence of society, took the resolution of writing no more, and bade adieu to his friends and epistolary correspondence, "Valete amici, valete epistolæ."

Petrarch died a very short time after despatching this letter. His biographers and contemporary authors are not agreed as to the day of his demise, but the probability seems to be that it was the 18th of July. Many writers of his life tell us that he expired in the arms of Lombardo da Serigo, whom Philip Villani and Gianozzo Manetti make their authority for an absurd tradition connected with his death. They pretend that when he breathed his last several persons saw a white cloud, like the smoke of incense, rise to the roof of his chamber, where it stopped for some time and then vanished, a miracle, they add, clearly proving that his soul was acceptable to God, and ascended to heaven. Giovanni Manzini gives a different account. He says that Petrarch's people found him in his library, sitting with his head reclining on a book. Having often seen him in this attitude, they were not alarmed at first; but, soon finding that he exhibited no signs of life, they gave way to their sorrow. According to Domenico Aretino, who was much attached to Petrarch, and was at that time at Padua, so that he may be regarded as good authority, his death was occasioned by apoplexy.

The news of his decease made a deep impression throughout Italy; and, in the first instance, at Arquà and Padua, and in the cities of the Euganean hills. Their people hastened in crowds to pay their last duties to the man who had honoured their country by his residence. Francesco da Carrara repaired to Arquà with all his nobility to assist at his obsequies. The Bishop went thither with his chapter and with all his clergy, and the common people flocked together to share in the general mourning.

The body of Petrarch, clad in red satin, which was the dress of the canons of Padua, supported by sixteen doctors on a bier covered with cloth of gold bordered with ermine, was carried to the parish church of Arquà, which was fitted up in a manner suitable to the ceremony. After the funeral oration had been pronounced by Bonaventura da Praga, of the order of the hermits of St. Augustin, the corpse was interred in a chapel which Petrarch himself had erected in the parish church in honour of the Virgin. A short time afterwards, Francesco Brossano, having caused a tomb of marble to be raised on four pillars opposite to the same church, transferred the body to that spot, and engraved over it an epitaph in some bad Latin lines, the rhyming of which is their greatest merit. In the year 1637, Paul Valdezucchi, proprietor of the house and grounds of Petrarch at Arquà, caused a bust of bronze to be placed above his mausoleum.

In the year 1630, his monument was violated by some sacrilegious thieves, who carried off some of his bones for the sake of selling them. The Senate of Venice severely punished the delinquents, and by their decree upon the subject testified their deep respect for the remains of this great man.

The moment the poet's will was opened, Brossano, his heir, hastened to forward to his friends the little legacies which had been left them; among the rest his fifty florins to Boccaccio. The answer of that most interesting man is characteristic of his sensibility, whilst it unhappily shows him to be approaching the close of his life (for he survived Petrarch but a year), in pain and extreme debility. "My first impulse," he says to Brossano, "on hearing of the decease of my master," so he always denominated our poet, "was to have hastened to his tomb to bid him my last adieu, and to mix my tears with yours. But ever since I lectured in public on the Divina Commedia of Dante, which is now ten months, I have suffered under a malady which has so weakened and changed me, that you would not recognise me. I have totally lost the stoutness and complexion which I had when you saw me at Venice. My leanness is extreme, my sight is dim, my hands shake, and my knees totter, so that I can hardly drag myself to my country-house at Certaldo, where I only languish. After reading your letter, I wept a whole night for my dear master, not on his own account, for his piety permits us not to doubt that he is now happy, but for myself and for his friends whom he has left in this world, like a vessel in a stormy sea without a pilot. By my own grief I judge of yours, and of that of Tullia, my beloved sister, your worthy spouse. I envy Arquà the happiness of holding deposited in her soil him whose heart was the abode of the Muses, and the sanctuary of philosophy and eloquence. That village, scarcely known to Padua, will henceforth be famed throughout the world. Men will respect it like Mount Pausilippo for containing the ashes of Virgil, the shore of the Euxine for possessing the tomb of Ovid, and Smyrna for its being believed to be the burial-place of Homer." Among other things, Boccaccio inquires what has become of his divine poem entitled Africa, and whether it had been committed to the flames, a fate with which Petrarch, from excess of delicacy, often threatened his compositions.

From this letter it appears that this epic, to which he owed the laurel and no small part of his living reputation, had not yet been published, with the exception of thirty-four verses, which had appeared at Naples through the indiscretion of Barbatus. Boccaccio said that Petrarch kept it continually locked up, and had been several times inclined to burn it. The author of the Decameron himself did not long survive his master: he died the 21st of December, 1375.

Petrarch so far succeeded in clearing the road to the study of antiquities, as to deserve the title which he justly retains of the restorer of classical learning; nor did his enthusiasm for ancient monuments prevent him from describing them with critical taste. He gave an impulse to the study of geography by his Itinerarium Syriacum. That science had been partially revived in the preceding century, by the publication of Marco Polo's travels, and journeys to distant countries had been accomplished more frequently than before, not only by religious missionaries, but by pilgrims who travelled from purely rational curiosity: but both of these classes of travellers, especially the religionists, dealt profusely in the marvellous; and their falsehoods were further exaggerated by copyists, who wished to profit by the sale of MSS. describing their adventures. As an instance of the doubtful wonders related by wayfaring men, may be noticed what is told of Octorico da Pordenone, who met, at Trebizond, with a man who had trained four thousand partridges to follow him on journeys for three days together, who gathered around like chickens when he slept, and who returned home after he had sold to the Emperor as many of them as his imperial majesty chose to select.

His treatise, "De Remediis utriusque Fortunæ" (On the Remedies for both Extremes of Fortune) was one of his great undertakings in the solitude of Vaucluse, though it was not finished till many years afterwards, when it was dedicated to Azzo Correggio. Here he borrows, of course, largely from the ancients; at the same time he treats us to some observations on human nature sufficiently original to keep his work from the dryness of plagiarism.

His treatise on "A Solitary Life" was written as an apology for his own love of retirement—retirement, not solitude, for Petrarch had the social feeling too strongly in his nature to desire a perfect hermitage. He loved to have a friend now and then beside him, to whom he might say how sweet is solitude. Even his deepest retirement in the "shut-up valley" was occasionally visited by dear friends, with whom his discourse was so interesting that they wandered in the woods so long and so far, that the servant could not find them to announce that their dinner was ready. In his rapturous praise of living alone, our poet, therefore, says more than he sincerely meant; he liked retirement, to be sure, but then it was with somebody within reach of him, like the young lady in Miss Porter's novel, who was fond of solitude, and walked much in Hyde Park by herself, with her footman behind her.

His treatise, "De Otio Religiosorum," was written in 1353, after an agreeable visit to his brother, who was a monk. It is a commendation of the monastic life. He may be found, I dare say, to exaggerate the blessing of that mode of life which, in proportion to our increasing activity and intelligence, has sunk in the estimation of Protestant society, so that we compare the whole monkish fraternity with the drones in a hive, an ignavum pecus, whom the other bees are right in expelling.

Though I shall never pretend to be the translator of Petrarch, I recoil not, after writing his Life, from giving a sincere account of the impression which his poetry produces on my mind. I have studied the Italian language with assiduity, though perhaps at a later period of my life than enables the ear to be *perfectly* sensitive to its harmony, for it is in youth, nay, almost in childhood alone, that the melody and felicitous expressions of any tongue can touch our deepest sensibility; but still I have studied it with pains—I believe I can thoroughly appreciate Dante; I can perceive much in Petrarch that is elevated and tender; and I approach the subject unconscious of the slightest splenetic prejudice.

I demur to calling him the first of modern poets who refined and dignified the language of love. Dante had certainly set him the example. It is true that, compared with his brothers of classical antiquity in love-poetry, he appears like an Abel of purity offering innocent incense at the side of so many Cains making their carnal sacrifices. Tibullus alone anticipates his tenderness. At the same time, while Petrarch is purer than those classical lovers, he is never so natural as they sometimes are when their passages are least objectionable, and the sun-bursts of his real, manly, and natural human love seem to me often to come to us straggling through the clouds of Platonism.

I will not expatiate on the *concetti* that may be objected to in many of his sonnets, for they are so often in such close connection with exquisitely fine thoughts, that, in tearing away the weed, we might be in danger of snapping the flower.

I feel little inclined, besides, to dwell on Petrarch's faults with that feline dilation of vision which sees in the dark what would escape other eyes in daylight, for, if I could make out the strongest critical case against him, I should still have to answer this question, "How comes it that Petrarch's poetry, in spite of all these faults, has been the favourite of the world for nearly five hundred years?"

So strong a regard for Petrarch is rooted in the mind of Italy, that his renown has grown up like an oak which has reached maturity amidst the storms of ages, and fears not decay from revolving centuries. One of the high charms of his poetical language is its pure and melting melody, a charm untransferable to any more northern tongue.

No conformation of words will charm the ear unless they bring silent thoughts of corresponding sweetness to the mind; nor could the most sonorous, vapid verses be changed into poetry if they were set to the music of the Spheres. It is scarcely necessary to say that Petrarch has intellectual graces of thought and spiritual felicities of diction, without which his tactics in the mere march of words would be a worthless skill.

The love of Petrarch was misplaced, but its utterance was at once so fervid and delicate, and its enthusiasm so enduring, that the purest minds feel justified in abstracting from their consideration the unhappiness of the attachment, and attending only to its devout fidelity. Among his deepest admirers we shall find women of virtue above suspicion, who are willing to forget his Laura being married, or to forgive the circumstance for the eloquence of his courtship and the unwavering faith of his affection. Nor is this predilection for Petrarch the result of female vanity and the mere love of homage. No; it is a wise instinctive consciousness in women that the offer of love to them, without enthusiasm, refinement, and *constancy*, is of no value at all. Without these qualities in their wooers, they are the slaves of the stronger sex. It is no wonder, therefore, that they are grateful to Petrarch for holding up the perfect image of a lover, and that they regard him as a friend to that passion, on the delicacy and constancy of which the happiness, the most hallowed ties, and the very continuance of the species depend.

In modern Italian criticism there are two schools of taste, whose respective partizans may be called the Petrarchists and the Danteists. The latter allege that Petrarch's amatory poetry, from its platonic and mystic character, was best suited to the age of cloisters, of dreaming voluptuaries, and of men living under tyrannical Governments, whose thoughts and feelings were oppressed and disguised. The genius of Dante, on the other hand, they say, appeals to all that is bold and natural in the human breast, and they trace the grand revival of his popularity in our own times to the re-awakened spirit of liberty. On this side of the question the most eminent Italian scholars and poets are certainly ranged. The most gifted man of that country with whom I was ever personally acquainted, Ugo Foscolo, was a vehement Danteist. Yet his copious memory was well stored with many a sonnet of Petrarch, which he could repeat by heart; and with all his Danteism, he infused the deepest tones of admiration into his recitation of the Petrarchan sonnets.

And altogether, Foscolo, though a cautious, is a candid admirer of our poet. He says, "The harmony, elegance, and perfection of his poetry are the result of long labour; but its original conceptions and pathos always sprang from the sudden inspiration of a deep and powerful passion. By an attentive perusal of all the writings of Petrarch, it may be reduced almost to a certainty that, by dwelling perpetually on the same ideas, and by allowing his mind to prey incessantly on itself, the whole train of his feelings and reflections acquired one strong character and tone, and, if he was ever able to suppress them for a time, they returned to him with increased violence; that, to tranquillize this agitated state of his mind, he, in the first instance, communicated in a free and loose manner all that he thought and felt, in his correspondence with his intimate friends; that he afterwards reduced these narratives, with more order and description, into Latin verse; and that he, lastly, perfected them with a greater profusion of imagery and more art in his Italian poetry, the composition of which at first served only, as he frequently says, to divert and mitigate all his afflictions. We may thus understand the perfect concord which prevails in Petrarch's poetry between Nature and Art; between the accuracy of fact and the magic of invention; between depth and perspicuity; between devouring passion and calm meditation. It is precisely because the poetry of Petrarch originally sprang from the heart that his passion never seems fictitious or cold, notwithstanding the profuse ornament of his style, or the metaphysical elevation of his thoughts."

I quote Ugo Foscolo, because he is not only a writer of strong poetic feeling as well as philosophic judgment, but he is pre-eminent in that Italian critical school who see the merits of Petrarch in no exaggerated light, but, on the whole, prefer Dante to him as a poet. Petrarch's love-poetry, Foscolo remarks, may be considered as the intermediate link between that of the classics and the moderns. * * * * Petrarch both feels like the ancient and philosophizes like the modern poets. When he paints after the manner of the classics, he is equal to them.

I despair of ever seeing in English verse a translation of Petrarch's Italian poetry that shall be adequate and popular. The term adequate, of course, always applies to the translation of genuine poetry in a subdued sense. It means the best that can be expected, after making allowance for that escape of etherial spirit which is inevitable in the transfer of poetic thoughts from one language to another. The word popular is also to be taken in a limited meaning regarding all translations. Cowper's ballad of John Gilpin is twenty times more popular than his Homer; yet the latter work is deservedly popular in comparison with the bulk of translations from antiquity. The same thing may be said of Cary's Dante; it is, like Cowper's Homer, as adequate and popular as translated poetry can be expected to be. Yet I doubt if either of those poets could have succeeded so well with Petrarch. Lady Dacre has shown much grace and ingenuity in the passages of our poet which she has versified; but she could not transfer into English those graces of Petrarchan diction, which are mostly intransferable. She could not bring the Italian language along with her.

Is not this, it may be asked, a proof that Petrarch is not so genuine a poet as Homer and Dante, since his charm depends upon the delicacies of diction that evaporate in the transfer from tongue to tongue, more than on hardy thoughts that will take root in any language to which they are transplanted? In a general view, I agree with this proposition; yet, what we call felicitous diction can never have a potent charm without refined thoughts, which, like essential odours, may be too impalpable to bear transfusion. Burns has the happiest imaginable Scottish diction; yet, what true Scotsman would bear to see him *done* into French? And, with the exception of German, what language has done justice to Shakespeare?

The reader must be a true Petrarchist who is unconscious of a general similarity in the character of his sonnets, which, in the long perusal of them, amounts to monotony. At the same time, it must be said that this monotonous similarity impresses the mind of Petrarch's reader exactly in proportion to the slenderness of his acquaintance with the poet. Does he approach Petrarch's sonnets for the first time, they will probably appear to him all as like to each other as the sheep of a flock; but, when he becomes more familiar with them, he will perceive an interesting individuality in every sonnet, and will discriminate their individual character as precisely as the shepherd can distinguish every single sheep of his flock by its voice and face. It would be rather tedious to pull out, one by one, all the sheep and lambs of our poet's flock of sonnets, and to enumerate the varieties of their bleat; and though, by studying the subject half his lifetime, a man might classify them by their main characteristics, he would find they defy a perfect classification, as they often blend different qualities. Some of them have a uniform expression of calm and beautiful feeling. Others breathe ardent and almost hopeful passion. Others again show him jealous, despondent, despairing; sometimes gloomily, and sometimes with touching resignation. But a great many of them have a mixed character, where, in the space of a line, he passes from one mood of mind to another.

As an example of pleasing and calm reflection, I would cite the first of his sonnets, according to the order in which they are usually printed. It is singular to find it confessing the poet's shame at the retrospect of so many years spent.

Voi ch' ascoltate in rime sparse il suono.

Ye who shall hear amidst my scatter'd lays
The sighs with which I fann'd and fed my heart.
When, young and glowing, I was but in part
The man I am become in later days;
Ye who have mark'd the changes of my style
From vain despondency to hope as vain,
From him among you, who has felt love's pain,
I hope for pardon, ay, and pity's smile,
Though conscious, now, my passion was a theme,
Long, idly dwelt on by the public tongue,
I blush for all the vanities I've sung,
And find the world's applause a fleeting dream.

The following sonnet (cxxvi.) is such a gem of Petrarchan and Platonic homage to beauty that I subjoin my translation of it with the most sincere avowal of my conscious inability to do it justice.

In what ideal world or part of heaven
Did Nature find the model of that face
And form, so fraught with loveliness and grace,

> In which, to our creation, she has given
> Her prime proof of creative power above?
> What fountain nymph or goddess ever let
> Such lovely tresses float of gold refined
> Upon the breeze, or in a single mind,
> Where have so many virtues ever met,
> E'en though those charms have slain my bosom's weal?
> He knows not love who has not seen her eyes
> Turn when she sweetly speaks, or smiles, or sighs,
> Or how the power of love can hurt or heal.

Sonnet lxix. is remarkable for the fineness of its closing thought.

> Time was her tresses by the breathing air
> Were wreathed to many a ringlet golden bright,
> Time was her eyes diffused unmeasured light,
> Though now their lovely beams are waxing rare,
> Her face methought that in its blushes show'd
> Compassion, her angelic shape and walk,
> Her voice that seem'd with Heaven's own speech to talk;
> At these, what wonder that my bosom glow'd!
> A living sun she seem'd—a spirit of heaven.
> Those charms decline: but does my passion? No!
> I love not less—the slackening of the bow
> Assuages not the wound its shaft has given.

The following sonnet is remarkable for its last four lines having puzzled all the poet's commentators to explain what he meant by the words "Al man ond' io scrivo è fatta arnica, a questo volta." I agree with De Sade in conjecturing that Laura in receiving some of his verses had touched the hand that presented them, in token of her gratitude.[15]

> In solitudes I've ever loved to abide
> By woods and streams, and shunn'd the evil-hearted,
> Who from the path of heaven are foully parted;
> Sweet Tuscany has been to me denied,
> Whose sunny realms I would have gladly haunted,
> Yet still the Sorgue his beauteous hills among
> Has lent auxiliar murmurs to my song,
> And echoed to the plaints my love has chanted.

> Here triumph'd, too, the poet's hand that wrote
> These lines—the power of love has witness'd this.
> Delicious victory! I know my bliss,
> She knows it too—the saint on whom I dote.

Of Petrarch's poetry that is not amatory, Ugo Foscolo says with justice, that his three political canzoni, exquisite as they are in versification and style, do not breathe that enthusiasm which opened to Pindar's grasp all the wealth of imagination, all the treasures of historic lore and moral truth, to illustrate and dignify his strain. Yet the vigour, the arrangement, and the perspicuity of the ideas in these canzoni of Petrarch, the tone of conviction and melancholy in which the patriot upbraids and mourns over his country, strike the heart with such force, as to atone for the absence of grand and exuberant imagery, and of the irresistible impetus which peculiarly belongs to the ode.

Petrarch's principal Italian poem that is not thrown into the shape of the sonnet is his Trionfi, or Triumphs, in five parts. Though not consisting of sonnets, however, it has the same amatory and constant allusions to Laura as the greater part of his poetry. Here, as elsewhere, he recurs from time to time to the history of his passion, its rise, its progress, and its end. For this purpose, he describes human life in its successive stages, omitting no opportunity of introducing his mistress and himself.

1. Man in his youthful state is the slave of love. 2. As he advances in age, he feels the inconveniences of his amatory propensities, and endeavours to conquer them by chastity. 3. Amidst the victory which he obtains over himself, Death steps in, and levels alike the victor and the vanquished. 4. But Fame arrives after death, and makes man as it were live again after death, and survive it for ages by his fame. 5. But man even by fame cannot live for ever, if God has not granted him a happy existence throughout eternity. Thus Love triumphs over Man; Chastity triumphs over Love; Death triumphs over both; Fame triumphs over Death; Time triumphs over Fame; and Eternity triumphs over Time.

The subordinate parts and imagery of the Trionfi have a beauty rather arabesque than classical, and resembling the florid tracery of the later oriental Gothic architecture. But the whole effect of the poem is pleasing, from the general grandeur of its design.

In summing up Petrarch's character, moral, political, and poetical, I should not stint myself to the equivocal phrase used by Tacitus respecting Agricola: *Bonum virum facile dixeris, magnum libenter*, but should at once claim for his memory the title both of great and good. A restorer of ancient learning, a rescuer of its treasures from oblivion, a despiser of many contemporary superstitions, a man, who, though no reformer himself, certainly contributed to the Reformation, an Italian patriot who was above provincial partialities, a poet who still lives in the hearts of his country, and who is shielded from oblivion by more generations than there were hides in the sevenfold shield of Ajax—if this was not a great man, many who are so called must bear the title unworthily. He was a faithful friend, and a devoted lover, and appears to have been one of the most fascinating beings that ever existed. Even when his failings were admitted, it must still be said that *even his failings leaned to virtue's side*, and, altogether we may pronounce that

> His life was gentle, and the elements
> So mix'd in him that Nature might stand up
> And say to all the world, "This was a man!"

---

[1] Before the publication of De Sade's "Mémoires pour la vie de Petrarque" the report was that Petrarch first saw Laura at Vaucluse. The truth of their first meeting in the church of St. Clara depends on the authenticity of the famous note on the M.S. Virgil of Petrarch, which is now in the Ambrosian Library at Milan.

[2] Petrarch, in his dialogue with St. Augustine, states that he was older than Laura by a few years.

[3] "The Floral games were instituted in France in 1324. They were founded by Clementina Isaure, Countess of Toulouse, and annually celebrated in the month of May. The Countess published an edict, which assembled all the poets of France, in artificial arbours, dressed with flowers; and he that produced the best poem was rewared with a violet of gold. There were, likewise, inferior prizes of flowers made in silver. In the meantime, the conquerors were crowned with natural chaplets of their own respective flowers. During the ceremony degrees were also conferred. He who had won a prize three times was pronounced a doctor '*en gaye science*,' the name of the poetry of the Provençal Troubadours. This institution, however fantastic, soon became common, through the whole of France."—*Warton's History of English Poetry*, vol i. p 467.

[4] I have transferred the following anecdote from Levati's Viaggi di Petrarea (vol. i. p. 119 et seq.). It behoves me to confess, however, that I recollect no allusion to it in any of Petrarch's letters, and I have found many things in Levati's book which make me distrust his authority.

[5] Quest' anima gentil che si disparte.—Sonnet xxiii.

[6] Dated 21st December. 1335.

[7] Guido Sette of Luni, in the Genoese territory, studied law together with Petrarch; but took to it with better liking. He devoted himself to the business of the bar at Avignon with much

reputation. But the legal and clerical professions were then often united; for Guido rose in the church to be an archbishop. He died in 1368, renowned as a church luminary.

[8] Canzoni 8, 9, and 10.

[9] Valery, in his "Travels in Italy" gives the following note respecting out poet. I quote from the edition of the work published at Brussels in 1835:—"Petrarque rapporte dans ses lettres latines que le laurier du Capitole lui avait attiré une multitude d'envieux; que le jour de son couronnement, au lieu d'eau odorante qu'il était d'usage de répandre dans ces solennités, il reçut sur la tête une eau corrosive, qui le rendit chauve le reste de sa vie. Son historien Dolce raconte même qu'une vieille lui jetta son pot de chambre rempli d'une acre urine, gardée, peut-être, pour cela depuis sept semaines."

[10] Sonnet cxcvi.

[11] *Translation.*—In the twenty-fifth year of his age, after a short though happy existence, our John departed this life in the year of Christ 1361, on the 10th of July, or rather on the 9th, at the midhour between Friday and Saturday. Sent into the world to my mortification and suffering, he was to me in life the cause of deep and unceasing solicitude, and in death of poignant grief. The news reached me on the evening of the 13th of the same month that he had fallen at Milan, in the general mortality caused by that unwonted scourge which at last discovered and visited so fearfully this hitherto exempted city. On the 8th of August, the same year, a servant of mine returning from Milan brought me a rumour (which on the 18th of the same fatal month was confirmed by a servant of *Dominus Theatinus*) of the death of my Socrates, my companion, my best of brothers, at Babylon (Avignon, I mean) in the month of May. I have lost my comrade and the solace of my life! Receive, Christ Jesus, these two, and the five that remain, into thy eternal habitations!

[12] Petrarch's words are: "civi servare suo;" but he takes the liberty of considering Charles as —adoptively—Italian, though that Prince was born at Prague.

[13] Most historians relate that the English, at Poitiers, amounted to no more than eight or ten thousand men; but, whether they consisted of eight thousand or thirty thousand, the result was sufficiently glorious for them, and for their brave leader, the Black Prince.

[14] This is the story of the patient Grisel, which is familiar in almost every language.

[15] Cercato ho sempre solitaria vita.—Sonnet 221, De Sade, vol. ii. p. 8.

This web edition published by:
eBooks@Adelaide
The University of Adelaide Library
University of Adelaide
South Australia 5005

Printed in Great Britain
by Amazon